P9-AOP-012

The
Imitation of Mary

Blessed are those who imitate our Lady,
for in imitating her they imitate Jesus.

IMITATION OF MARY

IN FOUR BOOKS

BY

ALEXANDER DE ROUVILLE

NEW ILLUSTRATED EDITION

Revised and Edited by
MATTHEW J. O'CONNELL

CATHOLIC BOOK PUBLISHING CORP.
NEW YORK

NIHIL OBSTAT: Richard T. Adams, M.A.
Censor Deputatus

IMPRIMATUR: ✠ James P. Mahoney, D.D.
Vicar General, Archdiocese of New York

(T-330)

ISBN 978-0-89942-330-2

PREFACE

NO sooner had the incomparable *Imitation of Christ* appeared than the faithful began spontaneously to wish for an *Imitation of Mary* that might be set beside Kempis' great work. Finally, a sixteenth-century Spanish Jesuit, Francisco Arias, published a little book entitled *The Imitation of Our Lady* (Valencia, 1588), and it seemed that the prayers of many devout souls had been answered. But the work was not what they were waiting for. It was a short pamphlet of twelve chapters that dealt in a very general way with the virtues of Mary and was in no way comparable to the great book that had already won the name of "Fifth Gospel."

The book here translated, on the contrary, was indeed what devotees of Mary had been looking for. It was published in French in 1768 and did not bear its author's name. Italian translations of a later date did, however, have an author's name on the title page: the Abbé d'Hérouville. Who was the Abbé d'Hérouville, and how is the initial anonymity to be explained?

The author was in fact a French Jesuit, Alexandre Joseph de Rouville (born at Lyons in

1716). After the Society of Jesus had been suppressed by Pope Clement XIV in 1773, he took the name Abbé d'Hérouville, thus assimilating himself, as far as title went, to the secular clergy. But even before the suppression by the Pope, Louis XIV had expelled the Society of Jesus from France in 1764; for this reason when the *Imitation of Mary* was first published in 1768 it had to appear anonymously.

The book quickly won a wide readership in France and Belgium and was translated into many languages. The first Italian translation, for example, was published at Padua in 1772, only four years after the book first appeared.

In the *Imitation of Mary* the author follows the Blessed Virgin through the different mysteries and circumstances of her life, from her Immaculate Conception to her Assumption into heaven. At each point he reflects on her conduct and her sentiments, thus providing instructive insights which will help every Christian in the varying situations of his or her own life.

In order to hold the reader's attention the author varies the manner in which he presents his reflections. Sometimes he speaks to God, sometimes to Mary, sometimes to the reader; at times he reflects as though he were by himself in meditation, and very often he has the Blessed Virgin speak to her child, the reader.

The order provided by the mysteries of Mary is pursued through the first three books. The fourth takes a different approach, but the devotees of Mary will be pleased that the author here tries to sum up in a few chapters the various aspects of devotion to the Mother of God and the various helps for fostering, maintaining, and reviving the sentiments of respect, love, and trust which her children ought to have for her.

The reader will not judge this book as though its author were claiming to rival the perfection of his model, Kempis' *Imitation of Christ*; he professed, on the contrary, to be fully satisfied if only his book were not totally unlike its model. In fact, however, if we judge by the devotion and solid piety toward God and His Blessed Mother which fill these pages, we must say that author has not been unworthy of his more famous forerunner.

CONTENTS

BOOK I

LIFE AND VIRTUES OF THE BLESSED VIRGIN MARY FROM HER IMMACULATE CONCEPTION TO THE BIRTH OF JESUS

Chapter	*Page*

BOOK II

LIFE AND VIRTUES OF THE BLESSED VIRGIN MARY FROM THE BIRTH OF HER DIVINE SON, JESUS, TO HIS DEATH

Chapter	*Page*

BOOK IV

OUR SENTIMENTS TOWARD MARY

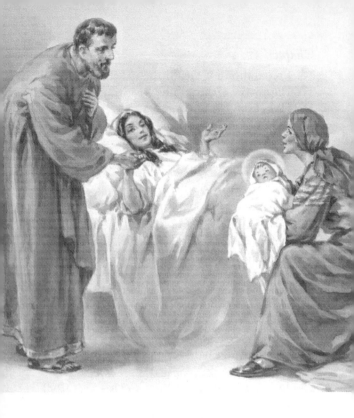

BIRTH OF THE BLESSED VIRGIN

Tradition tells us that a holy couple, St. Joachim and St. Ann, had no children for a long time. When God answered their prayers and gave them a daughter, they named her Mary, which means Lady or Star of the Sea.

BOOK 1

*Life and Virtues of the Blessed Virgin Mary
from Her Immaculate Conception
to the Birth of Jesus*

CHAPTER 1

IMITATION OF THE VIRTUES OF THE BLESSED VIRGIN

BLESSED *those who do not abandon the way
I have bidden them go! Blessed those who
listen to what I tell them* (Prov 8:32-33) and who
follow the models of virtue I offer them.

In putting these words on the lips of Mary,
the Church urges us to study the life of the
Queen of Saints and to imitate her splendid
example.

Happy the man who imitates our Lady, for
in imitating her he imitates Jesus, king and
incomparable model of all virtue.

The Blessed Virgin's life contains lessons
for everyone. If we study it, we learn how to
live in prosperity and adversity, prayer and
work, honors and humiliations.

We shall never attain the perfection she
brought to every action; but our perfection can
be measured by our closeness to her.

You claim to be the servants of Mary: do you really want to become like her in her sublime holiness? Then imitate, as far as you can, her lively faith, her prompt obedience, her deep humility, her selfless intentions, her generous love.

Is there any one of you that cannot make it your aim, with the help of God's grace, to follow Mary's example in the practice of these virtues?

Without such imitation your love for her will be a weak thing indeed, and you cannot expect to receive evident proof of her special protection.

True enough, you recite daily prayers in her honor; you give external signs of your devotion to her; you belong to a society that is especially consecrated to her. And all this binds her to ask God for the saving graces you need.

But if your devotion does not take you a step further and lead you to imitate her virtues, then your devotion will not save you.

The Philistines took possession of the ark of the Lord and adorned it with their gifts. But the ark did not become a source of blessing for them, because they continued to adore their idols as before.

O Queen of all the virtues, is it not fitting that one who loves you should do for you what he does for his friends in this world?

We try to adapt ourselves to our friends' character and to make their likes and dislikes our own. Such adaptation leads to a union of hearts. In fact, we may say that where there is no likeness there can be no friendship.

Your heart, Blessed Virgin, is utterly humble, pure, submissive to God's will, and zealous for His interests. How can it be united in the bonds of affection to a heart that is pleasure-seeking, proud, unresigned to God's will, and without zeal for His glory?

The Apostle rightly says: *"If you love me, then imitate me as I imitate Jesus"* (1 Cor 4:16). If you are really my children (Mary says), then make your mother's spirit your own: the spirit of charity, peace, self-denial, and reverent love for God.

Holy Virgin, from now on I will show you my loving devotion by imitating your virtues. There is no greater homage, no greater proof of love, that I can give.

CHAPTER 2

ESTEEM OF SANCTIFYING GRACE

MARY was free of original sin from the very first moment of her existence; she possessed the grace of God in the very instant of her conception.

All of us come into this world as the unfortunate victims of God's anger; Mary alone was protected from the very beginning by God's love and so came into this world as a masterpiece of grace.

God did not want the temple in which He was to dwell to be soiled in any way. The Son's honor required that His Mother not be even for a single moment the slave of Satan.

How Mary must have valued the incomparable favor done her. In her eyes that favor was, as wisdom had been for Solomon, *the source of all blessings* (Prov 8:18).

The Lord possessed her from the beginning of His ways (Prov 8:22). That is what Mary valued more than anything earth could offer. She had many other prerogatives given her by God, but this first favor was more precious than all the rest, since it brought her closer to God. Her life in its entirety was continuous expression of gratitude to Him for a gift which she shared with no other pure creature.

Christian soul, in baptism you received the sanctifying grace that Mary received in the moment of conception. That grace brought you the right to call God your father and Jesus your brother. You became *an heir of God and a coheir with Christ Jesus* (Rom 8:17). The kingdom of heaven itself was set aside as your inheritance.

Do you fully understand what a great and glorious privilege is yours? And do you understand all the duties it lays upon you?

Alas! How few Christians even reflect on this privilege! How few try to live holy lives and thus prove worthy of the dignity that is theirs! How few make an effort to keep unspotted the baptismal garment of sinlessness that marks the innocent, pure, and loving child of God!

On the contrary, we often take pride in the honors bestowed by the world and, in an extraordinary inversion of values, put grace last, even though it is the only thing that, properly speaking, deserves our respect and esteem.

Many take pride in not being unworthy descendants of a supposedly illustrious lineage. At the same time, however, they are not afraid to betray their spiritual descent from God by an unclean life given over to the pleasures of the senses. They boast of an independence that is in fact an illusion, but are not ashamed to enter into a horrible partnership with the devil and thus to accept his dominion once again, to put on his uniform once more, and to return to the condition of slavery in which they had the misfortune of being born.

They eagerly pursue earthly goods and neglect, or even scorn, the everlasting heritage of heavenly blessings set aside for them!

Ungrateful hearts, pitiful victims of sin, whoever you may be, *at least do not close your hearts to God's voice as He calls out to you* (Ps 95:7-8).

You can regain the grace of adoption which you threw away, for there is a second baptism: the baptism of penance. Make use of it with trust and assurance, for your heavenly Father's greatest desire is to make you His friends once more. But use it quickly. Who knows but that a short time from now you may no longer be able to do so!

Pure and spotless Virgin, pray for us, that we may stop sinning, that we may sin no more, that we may persevere in our intention of making up for the great harm done by our sins.

Your intercession will win us the grace of perfect friendship with God. Therefore, we shall be able to praise you for being, after your Son Jesus, the source of our salvation.

CHAPTER 3

DILIGENCE IN PRESERVING
SANCTIFYING GRACE

MARY was conceived in God's grace; there was no trace of sin in her nor any inclination to sin. Therefore, unlike us, she had no reason to fear falling into sin. Yet, if you were to judge by the way she acted, you would say that she had as much reason to fear it as we do, or even more than we do!

She watched constantly over her own heart as though creatures could have drawn her affections to themselves. She watched over her every word as though she could not trust her tongue.

In her conception she was given all the privileges that go with sinlessness, yet she decided to live permanently as a penitent!

We, on the contrary, are surrounded by flattering, treacherous enemies whose sole aim is to use our natural weakness to bring about our fall. Yet we have no fear and are not watchful at all!

We admit that we are weakness incarnate, yet frequently we expose ourselves to temptations that would bring down even the strongest soul.

When weakness is compounded by presumption, does it not deserve to lose all that supports it and gives it strength?

We carry the treasure of grace in a very weak vessel (2 Cor 4:7), that can shatter when we least expect it.

How many enemies are trying to snatch this treasure from us? Enemies within, enemies outside, enemies all around us.

Within us, there are the passions we have not sufficiently mastered; outside, the spirit of darkness; around us, a corrupt world. Like a flame not fully extinguished, our passions can always be rekindled and light a fire.

Even if we were, like St. Paul, *caught up to the third heaven* (2 Cor 12:2), we would still have to fear being cast down with the rebellious angels into the bottomless abyss.

It is not enough to assure ourselves that our sentiments are heartfelt and our resolutions fervent.

A single inopportune occasion is enough to destroy us. A single glance deprived David of the Lord's love. A Delilah can destroy even a Samson.

The holiest pillars have fallen after struggling for many years against violent temptations.

When we travel the road of virtue, one day does not guarantee the next; after receiving many graces from the Lord a person may through unfaithfulness be rejected by Him.

The man who relies on his own past resolutions and does not keep close watch on himself will soon be unfaithful to them.

Anyone who tries to cross a stormy sea with hidden reefs and does not take all the necessary precautions must expect a quick and tragic shipwreck.

It is hard, I admit, to be forced to live in continual watchfulness over our inclinations so that we may overcome them; but no one has ever become a saint without vigilance and struggle.

My God! Fill me with holy fear of You! Then I shall be watchful, and my watchfulness will win for me the strength to emerge victorious from all my struggles.

Teach me fully to understand how the grace that makes us Your friends and Your children is the only good that deserves my deep concern, the only good whose loss should cause me sorrow. Happy indeed shall I be if I never lose this priceless treasure! For then I shall be spared many anxieties during this life, and shall have piled up riches for the life to come.

Happy shall I be, happy beyond compare, if I remain faithful to my intention of putting up with every evil rather than expose myself to the danger of losing Your grace!

If I can guard this treasure, You will dwell in my soul. You will possess it by Your presence, enlighten it with Your wisdom, support it by Your power, give it constant proofs of Your tender love, and be Yourself its reward in time and eternity.

CHAPTER 4

DILIGENCE IN GROWING IN GRACE AND PERFECTION

The Believer

FROM the very moment of your conception, Holy Virgin, you received the fullness of grace. Yet you were not satisfied to sit back and enjoy this great blessing; instead, your entire life was a continuous effort to make it bear fruit.

In turn, since grace is intensified wherever effort is made, it enriched you more and more each day.

You were a carefully cultivated soil, in which even the smallest seed bore fruit a hundredfold.

Though you were entirely holy at birth, that holiness, even for you, was not a natural endowment; yet you made it seem almost a part of nature through your actions and diligent care.

Mary *put forth branches like the palm tree and spread them everywhere; they are branches of honor and grace* (Sir 24:16).

Mary

My child, if you want to grow in the grace that makes you a friend and child of God, a temple of the Holy Spirit, a brother of Christ and a coheir with Him, then flee the world, love prayer, receive the sacraments often, and apply yourself to the practice of the virtues proper to your state.

One very special means of increasing habitual grace in yourself is to be faithful to the inspirations brought by actual grace. Listen to the voice that speaks within you and be guided by its urgings. The more you listen to it, the more it will teach you. The more you advance, the more it will teach you to do new and greater things.

Many walk for a while in the path of virtue but then are satisfied with the distance they have gone. But grace never says: "Enough!"

Others think they are doing a great deal if they do not slip into evil. Yet that is not enough; for the good man must strive daily to become better.

Many a Christian will be surprised on the day of judgment to see himself heavily in debt to God's justice because he did not make use of the means given him for becoming a great saint!

On the path of virtue, not to advance is to go backwards; not to gain is to lose.

When we set limits to our service of God, God does not respond by setting limits to His benefits. On the other hand, the more generous we are toward Him, the more generous and liberal He will be toward us, even in this life.

However few our treasures in this world, they are always sufficient; but we can never have too many of the benefits of grace.

The servant who fails to take care of the possessions his master has entrusted to him will be punished. Therefore, shake off your sluggishness, my child, for it may turn into a deadly lethargy. Try to make up for lost time. Stop saying you are satisfied with the last place *in the heavenly Father's house* (Jn 14:2); for if you talk that way you run the risk of having no place at all.

The Believer

Mary, you are a powerful and zealous defender! Help me to live in holiness the life God gave me solely that I might devote it to loving and serving Him! Help me reach that glory which I must win through God's grace and my own efforts and which will be proportioned to the fervor of those efforts.

CHAPTER 5

WE MUST GIVE OURSELVES TO GOD WHILE ON EARTH

LISTEN, *my daughter, with care to what I shall say to you: Forget your people and your father's house* (Ps 45:11), and you shall win the heart of the king which you have touched. That king is your God.

During her life on earth Mary listened to the voice of God that called her into solitude; from her earliest years she left her father's house and consecrated herself to God in the temple. Nothing could hold her back: not youthfulness nor bodily weakness nor love of parents.

Everything that delays the sacrifice of a heart which seeks and loves God alone, afflicts that heart, for it also delays its happiness.

Once she became an inhabitant of the temple, Mary fulfilled in the most perfect way possible the duties that were entrusted to her in accordance with her age and strength.

She devoted to prayer and meditation the time left to her; that is how she prepared herself for the very special graces God was to give her.

O daughter of heaven's king, how noble and splendid are the first steps you take! (Song 7:2).

Others will follow your example. "In your train countless virgins will joyfully consecrate themselves in the temple of the king of kings." The offering they will make to the God of their youth, their heart, their freedom, their entire self, will be an act of perfect homage to His majesty; and the homage will be a source of blessings which He shall heap upon them throughout their lives.

What self-deception to think that the young are not capable of virtue!

Mary and the Saints have shown us how profitable it is for a man *to have carried the yoke of the Lord from his very youth* (Lam 3:27).

Do we treat God as God when we give Him only the shabby remnants of a life that was given us that we might spend it wholly in His service? What kind of a sacrifice are we offering to God when we wait to commit ourselves to His service until, by worldly standards, we have neither strength nor means left?

Do not wait until old age to give yourself to God. By that time we are exhausted from the world's yoke and have no strength left to carry God's yoke.

You say you will give yourself to God when you are older. But when will that day come? And when it comes, will you succeed in turning to God as easily as you think?

Experience teaches us that mature years bring knowledge but not necessarily wisdom.

Lord! Lord! Open the door for us! (Mt 25:11), cried the foolish virgins but they came too late and knocked on the door in vain.

Experience teaches us that maturer years make us ready to enter the presence of the supreme judge, Who asks an account of one's whole life!

The man who does not consecrate to God the early years of his life may well fear that to punish him God may allow his life to be long drawn out.

My God, how many know You but do not love You! I should be inconsolable at the thought. But, if I am easily consoled, can I at least say that I have at last begun to love You?

If I were only a child once again! I would want mind and heart, thoughts and affections, everything in me, to be given to You.

Thank You for Your great mercy in preserving my life while I spent it in offending You.

I beg for Your grace! May it help me to serve You until my dying breath, and to serve You all the more faithfully as I have begun so late to be Your servant.

CHAPTER 6

WE MUST GIVE OURSELVES TO GOD ENTIRELY AND FOREVER

The Believer

FERVENT Virgin, you consecrated yourself to God during this life, and you did it without reservation or restriction.

You surrendered your liberty to Him in its entirety, that you might have no will but His.

The only satisfaction you wanted in this world was that of pleasing Him; the only pleasure, that of depriving yourself, for love of Him, of every pleasure.

You never broke your promise; you walked the path God showed you and every day made new progress.

Your example condemns my fickleness in God's service and my reservations toward Him.

I am ashamed of my behavior. For God is ever the same toward me and deserves from me a like devotion and fidelity.

Mary

My child, why did you stop after beginning so well? Is God no longer the great and lovable master He once was? Has the relationship between you changed? Do you perhaps depend on Him less at one season than another? Is not your duty to give yourself entirely to Him the same at every moment?

As you advance in years, God's benefits also become more numerous; your gratitude and, therefore, your fidelity ought also grow.

God alone created your heart, and He created it for Himself alone. He alone should be its master.

He did not say: "Lend Me your heart," but: *Give Me your heart* (Prov 23:26). You obeyed Him and consecrated your heart to Him. What right did you have to take it back?

You do the world far too much honor when you give it a share in your affections.

You insult God greatly when you confront Him with such a rival.

You say you would regard it as the greatest misfortune not to be among the friends of God. But can this jealous God call Himself the friend of someone so lukewarm and slothful?

God does not think it too much that He should give Himself entirely to you. Live your life, therefore, entirely for Him. Give Him all and in Him you will find all.

The world and all it contains is as nothing to the man for whom God is everything.

The Believer

I am weak, holy Virgin, and need a great and powerful grace if I am to profit by your instruction and to walk in your footsteps.

Win for me, I beg you, the help I need, even while you encourage me by your fervent example.

After such inconstancy and infidelity, shall I dare offer my heart again to Jesus? But His anger must give way to *a contrite and humble heart* (Ps 51:19). But above all it must give way to your meditating prayer.

Mother of mercy (the liturgy), enable me to make my peace with Him. May God my Savior, at your prayer, so fill my heart with His grace that in serving so good a master I shall place no limits, know no hesitation, and yearn for Him alone.

CHAPTER 7

THE ADVANTAGES AND DELIGHTS OF SOLITUDE

The Believer

HOLY Virgin, in the temple your days were intensely peaceful and calm.

In tranquility and leisure you enjoyed the visitations of God and prepared within your-

MARY IS OFFERED IN THE TEMPLE

When Mary was three years old, tradition tells us, her parents took her to the Temple to offer her to God. She may have lived in the Temple until the age of twelve, working as a servant girl.

self a dwelling-place for Him that was ever more splendid and worthy of Him.

The thought of God's presence with you was always before your mind. You were ceaselessly preoccupied with the contemplation of His greatness and perfections.

Your beloved was everything to you, and you to Him (Song 2:16). Compared with Him the world's wealth and beauty were as nothing in your eyes.

Mary

My child, the soul that is detached from the world and all that occupies the world lives truly happy days in solitude. Its only concern is with God, as though it were alone on earth with Him.

In solitude the spirit is always recollected so that it may hear the Lord's voice, and nothing can interrupt the heart's own voice as it constantly speaks to God.

It delights in repeating the simple words, *You are the God of my heart* (Ps 73:26), and finds in them its whole fulfillment, wealth, and joy.

Seated, like the spouse in the Song of Songs, *in the shadow of the beloved* (Song 2:3), the soul looks with compassion on men as they take so many sorrows on themselves in order to become great and rich, for it cannot understand how men can love aught but Him Whom it loves.

Whatever may happen on this earth, the soul is not disturbed. For the beloved has always been and always will be holy and lovable, and this thought provides ever new reason for rejoicing.

When God wants to teach divine lessons to a soul and *speak to her heart, He leads her into the desert* (Hos 2:16).

Think, my child, what a taste for solitude and spirit of recollection the Saints must have had! Find your delight, then, in living far from the world and pay no heed to yourself apart from necessity. And when necessity does force you to take heed, be like the dove that, when forced to leave the ark, returned immediately because outside it could find no place to alight.

If you are not careful to flee the world, it will soon beguile you, and once you have tasted what the world has to offer, you will no longer have any taste for what God offers.

The spouse in the Song of Songs sought her beloved on the streets of Jerusalem and could not find him.

Bear in mind that never yet have you had dealings with the world without being worse off in God's eyes than when you began.

You must love solitude if you are safely to appear among men. For it is in solitude that you learn to act when you are amid the world.

To live withdrawn from the world is one of the most effective means of preserving your own innocence of soul. Nothing weakens a man's virtue more than the frequent companionship of men.

Can anyone breathe the poisoned air of the world without being infected by it? Pull back often into solitude and breathe its purer air.

The holy hermits tell us that they were never better able to converse intimately with God than when they had withdrawn from worldly affairs and worldly company.

My child, God finds His delight in being with you; find yours in being with Him in solitude.

There, far more freely than elsewhere, you can reveal to Him your inmost thoughts. You can far more readily manifest your feelings with the freedom that a respectful trust in Him will give you.

There, too, you will more easily develop the thoughts that will alleviate your sorrows, calm your fears, dissipate your doubts, and show you the sure way to act wisely in every situation.

Finally, it is in solitude that God enables your heart to hear the secret words that only

He can speak. His heart will speak to yours in a language that only His friends can understand, and His words will imprint upon your soul the truths that spring from His love.

CHAPTER 8

CHOICE OF A STATE OF LIFE

MARY sought God and loved Him alone from her earliest years. For this reason she drew down upon herself all His blessings, and He on His part provided a suitable state of life for her so that she might carry out His plans for her.

To make the right choice of a vocation we need a conjunction of events and circumstances such as Providence ordinarily provides for faithful souls who consult God on the choice of a state of life.

Can a young man hope that God will bestow this favor on him if he meanwhile is abandoning himself to the deadly urges of his own newfound passions?

By means of her marriage to St. Joseph, God in His providence enabled Mary to gather the previous fruit of the virtues she had practiced so faithfully.

If it had been left to the world to choose a husband for Mary, it would undoubtedly have chosen a rich and talented man.

It would not have thought of choosing a virtuous man, a man who from childhood had lived reverently before God. That is not the way the world thinks. Self-interest and purely human considerations are the motivating forces behind most marriages. The possessions which chance bestows, rather than the blessings of grace, lead to the contracting of marriages. The result is the many marriages between ill-suited partners, each of whom is the other's torment.

God permits this to happen as an earthly punishment for those who do not consult Him on so important a matter, a matter that can have a deadly outcome if not guided by Him.

He permits it as a punishment for the youthful carelessness that makes men fail to match the protestation of virtue with its practice.

The choice by Mary's parents, or rather by God, fell upon Joseph, *a just man* (Mt 1:19), in fact the most virtuous man then living on earth and the one most worthy to be the holy Virgin's husband.

No marriage ever turned out more happily; never were two hearts more delighted at their union. What trials could ever disturb their peace of soul! Mary and Joseph were in the state of life God wanted for them.

Many are dissatisfied with their state. They suffer a great deal from it and often make others suffer as well. And the reason is that they are in a state God did not want for them.

It is to such people that the prophet speaks: *Woe to you, children that have abandoned My providential care and made plans without consulting Me* (Isa 30:1).

A vocation is an important grace that includes many others. Be unfaithful to that grace and you cannot expect the others.

If you refuse this special providence which provides extraordinary graces for the person who is disposed to follow the Divine will, you fall under an ordinary providence which provides only ordinary graces with which indeed you can be saved, but with greater difficulty.

Pray to the Lord, therefore, and consult Him if you are deciding on a state of life. Say to Him with the prophet: *Show me the way You want me to walk* (Ps 143:8).

Live so that the Lord may see in you a fit subject for His special care.

If the Lord's will is not clear to you, consult those who on earth are His representatives; they will enlighten you on what you should do.

Jesus struck Saul to the earth on the road to Damascus, yet He did not directly make known to him His plans for him; instead, He sent him to Ananias who would reveal them to him.

Consult your parents only insofar as duty may require this. For it is always to be feared that they may give their children advice inspired by the principles of the world: *one's enemies will be the members of his own household* (Mt 10:36).

Finally, consult death, as it were. That is, make the choice you will wish you had made as your life is drawing to its end.

CHAPTER 9

PURITY AND THE ESTEEM YOU SHOULD HAVE FOR IT

WHEN the angel bids Mary become the Mother of God, he does not immediately explain how this great privilege is consistent with the vow of virginity she had made. Mary delays her consent, for she prefers to be the greatest of creatures in virginity rather than in dignity.

But *do not be afraid*, Mary (Lk 1:30), for it is this very chastity which you guard so carefully that will bring into your womb the God Who willed to be born only of a virgin.

Thus Mary gave her consent only after being informed by the angel that, as far as her virginity was concerned, she had nothing to fear in becoming the Mother of God.

Virginity was what made *the beloved disciple* (Jn 19:26) worthy of Jesus' special love. Happy the souls whom virginity adorned during their earthly life! They will have the incomparable privilege of *following the Lamb* in eternal life (Rev 14:4).

The prince of the Apostles was granted great privileges, yet it was only the virgin disciple that Jesus allowed to rest his head on His breast at the last supper. Jesus gave Peter the care of the Church; but to John He gave the care of His own Mother.

Through chastity we live on earth the life the blessed live in heaven.

The practice of this virtue wins us merits even the angels cannot have.

It is the most chaste souls that share most fully in the union which the Incarnate Word enters into with men.

All you who think the vice contrary to chastity is readily to be forgiven because our nature is weak, remember that it is one of the vices God has most reluctantly pardoned and most severely punished.

This vice drives away the divine spirit, which, Scripture tells us, does not "dwell in the carnal man." It is a vice which blinds a man. It took a prophet to make David the adulterer under-stand the enormity of his offense and think of doing penance.

It is a vice which hardens a man. Solomon was a marvelously wise man for many years, yet at the end of his life he became an idolater because he had become unchaste. *Our bodies are the temples of the Holy Spirit* (1 Cor 6:19). In a Christian, therefore, impurity is *the abomination that desolates the holy place* (Mt 24:15).

Jesus, spouse of virgins, You chose a Virgin for Your Mother. Grant me a tender love for chastity and the greatest possible horror of the vice that is its contrary.

The virtue of chastity is beyond the powers of our nature. *I cannot live chastely without a special grace.*

I ask of You the grace of that same chastity that made Mary so pleasing in Your sight and won her the honor of having You as her Son.

In asking it, I plead the love so many virgins have had for You, virgins who during their earthly lives loved only the beauty of the Divine Spouse.

Teach me to find my supreme pleasure in overcoming the pleasures Your law condemns.

Rouse in me a fear of those eternal fires You have prepared for the unchaste.

Extinguish in me all taste for sensual pleasures and grant me a taste for the joys of heaven. Free me from those wearying temptations that have thus far kept me company in the practice of piety.

If You think it necessary to let those temptations continue, then, my Savior, grant that I may fight against them unceasingly and profit by them to show my love for You.

CHAPTER 10

PRECAUTIONS FOR PRESERVING CHASTITY

BY REASON of her Immaculate Conception Mary was not open to the attacks of vice. And yet *she was greatly troubled* (Lk 1:29) at the sight of the angel who appeared to her in human form.

The angel greeted her, and immediately she *wondered what this greeting meant* (Lk 1:29).

She was alone with the angel; there were no witnesses. That was enough to rouse a holy fear in her.

"You shall bring forth a Son," the angel said, *"and give Him the name Jesus"* (Lk 1:31).

She did not doubt the possibility of what the angel was saying, *for nothing is impossible with God* (Lk 1:37). She asks only how the mystery will take place.

How discreet her question is! How modest! She says no more and no less than is required.

Here you may recognize a soul that makes purity its treasure.

Like a delicate flower, it fears the least breeze. A glance, even a single glance, and it is on guard.

A virgin who is well aware of the value of this virtue fears even the more remote occasions that can lead to some offense against it.

Flattery, engaging manners, innocent-sounding conversation: all these are suspect to such a soul and cause it to double its watchfulness and attention.

But if such precautions as these are necessary in order to preserve chastity in its full splendor, can we say that there are many chaste souls on earth?

It is greatly to be desired that men would devote to the genuine preservation of this virtue all the care they give to presenting the appearance of it!

How many people fall through idleness and an easy life, through dangerous reading, and through conversations that are too free!

Many Christian virgins converse frequently, and without any fear, with persons who are far from being angels.

They say they are watchful with regard to their virginity, but they fail to realize that the devil is also on the lookout to destroy them.

A virgin who loves praise will not long remain indifferent to the person who bestows the praise.

Where purity is concerned there is every reason to fear, precisely because we never fear enough.

We try not to see the danger in things we love. The proof that we love the danger is the effort we make to keep it hidden.

We are all formed of the same dust. Like so many others we too may learn through sad experience our own weakness.

We can trust greatly in the help of grace, but this does not allow us to expose ourselves to danger.

That help is guaranteed only to those who find themselves tempted without having sought temptation out.

You may have overcome the enemies of purity for many years, but do not think that you are therefore invincible. Continue to be distrustful of all things, even of yourself.

Be faithful in avoiding the daily occasions that lurk on every side; the devil is always ready to multiply them.

Then God will give you the gift of fortitude in facing the occasions you could not foresee, in which great virtue is needed if you are to overcome.

Prayer

Virgin Mother of God, win for me the grace to distrust myself, to be prudent in action, and to mortify my senses; for all these are needed if I am to continue to be chaste.

I cannot flatter myself that I belong (as indeed I wish to belong) among those who love you, if I do not love in a very special way this virtue that was the source of all your greatness.

"Mother pure and chaste, Queen of virgins" (Liturgy), win for me the grace of a delicate purity. Then you will always find in me the mark that distinguishes your dearest children.

CHAPTER 11

TRUE GREATNESS

THERE is an infinite difference between the distinctive marks the world recognizes and those which spring from grace.

Immense wealth, proud palaces, and countless servants bear witness to the king's greatness. Scorn for the world, a horror of sin, and the love of God show the greatness of the holy individual.

A man's authentic splendor and merit consist in his reverencing God and obeying His commandments.

The angel whom the Lord sent to Mary said to her: *"Hail, full of grace! The Lord is with you"* (Lk 1:28).

Could anything more glorious be said of this virgin?

Surely, all praise from men and angels is due her to whom it could be said: *"You have found grace before God"* (Lk 1:30); you are acceptable in His eyes.

At the time when the angel was sent to Mary, Augustus and Herod occupied royal thrones. Everyone vied in calling them great, powerful, liberal. But what were these kings in God's sight, Who alone is the judge of true greatness?

A young virgin, hidden in the solitude of Nazareth, was infinitely more worthy of such praises and truly deserved all these laudatory names.

True greatness is not to be measured according to the empty norms men use but according to the norms of God. He alone is great in Himself, and in His sight nothing is great except by relation to Him.

Of what value are all the heroes the world admires, as compared with the great men religion produces through the practice of virtue?

It is a more splendid thing to conquer one's own passions than to conquer nations.

It is much less difficult to conquer others than to conquer oneself.

The true Christian is not the kind of hero who owes his heroism to circumstances; he is not the accidental hero of a passing hour but a hero throughout a lifetime.

His glory is that he overcomes the obstacles in his path; his goal is to possess God and find rest in Him. Can there be a greater honor than to serve God and belong to Him? "To serve God is to rule."

When Scripture speaks of Abraham, Moses, and David—the greatest men our earth has known—it calls them servants of God. This single title includes all others; or, to speak more accurately, all the others are as naught compared with it.

The title of servant of God is as much superior to those of king and sovereign as God is to all the kings and powerful men of earth.

Immortal king, omnipotent Lord of the universe, I exist entirely for You and for You alone! Is it possible to know You and yet give Your honors to another? Is it possible to know You and not value beyond all else the privilege of serving You?

What a great honor for man, such a wretched thing in himself, that he can seek the honor of loving and serving You!

Lord, by Your grace enable me to understand how a person who lives a humble, obscure life, as Mary did, and tries to do Your will and serve You faithfully, accomplishes something far greater and more glorious than anything the blind and stupid world calls great and glorious.

May the nobility, honor, and glory that Your service brings inspire me, in all my duties and actions, to a greatness of soul, a generosity, and a constancy worthy of the Lord I serve.

CHAPTER 12

GOD'S GRACE IS FOR THE HUMBLE

Mary

MY CHILD, here is a secret way of obtaining great favors from God: regard yourself always as unworthy of His grace. *God gives His grace to the humble* (1 Pet 5:5). God finds no room for His favors in a heart that is full of itself.

The Believer

Queen of Saints, what profound instruction your words contain!

To see how humble you were, I need only consider how you acted when Gabriel the archangel came to you.

The angel told you that you had been chosen to be the Mother of God. You did not understand how God could have chosen you for such a sublime dignity.

The idea of such an immense elevation, high above nature, caused you as it were to suspect the angel's visit.

From the very moment when the supreme Being enclosed Himself in your womb, you thought only of immersing yourself in your nothingness.

Of the many titles connected with the dignity bestowed on you you kept only one: *servant of the Lord* (Lk 1:38).

How different you, the new Eve, were from the first Eve! Pride caused her to lose all her privileges; humility was the source of yours.

When He wanted to effect great and wonderful things in you, the Almighty did not look to your natural gifts nor to the splendor of your ancestry, but only to your humility.

It was only natural that a God who determined to humble Himself to the utmost should take an infinite delight in humility.

It was only right that He should choose as His mother a woman who by her humility merited the highest of all dignities.

Mary, you pleased God by your virginity, but you conceived Him by your humility.

Mary

My child, the Lord sees the greatest merit in a person who in his humility believes he has no merits, great though his merits may in fact be.

Upon what does God most gladly fix His gaze, whether in heaven or on earth? The humble soul.

He Himself says: *"To whom shall the Lord turn His gaze, if not to the poor man, the man of humble heart?"* (Ps 11:5—Vulgate).

Pride impoverishes many Christians and deprives them of the blessings of grace.

If they made an effort to know themselves, the knowledge would make them humble and humility would bring healing for their need through the graces it would obtain.

Empty yourself of self, my child, and God will fill you with His gifts. Enrich yourself by admitting that of yourself you can only be wretched.

If you are humble, God will use you to glorify Himself. He entrusts concern for His glory to those who have no desire to usurp it or to claim a share of it for themselves.

When you receive a favor from God, be humble and thankful that He is good enough to bestow continual favors on the least of His servants.

Attribute nothing to your own resources: neither the goods you possess nor anything you do.

Even when you correspond very faithfully to graces received, remember that it is only grace itself which enables you to be faithful and that in rewarding your fidelity God is but crowning His own gifts.

Keep three thoughts always present before you: God is all and I am nothing; God possesses everything and my only inheritance is wretchedness; God can do everything and I can do nothing without His help.

Then, even though you are nothing and possess nothing and can do nothing by your own powers, you will indeed be something in God's eyes. He will delight to give you His gifts and will make you victorious over all your enemies.

CHAPTER 13

CHRISTIAN HUMILITY IS TRUE GLORY

THE angel's words to Mary did not reflect her thoughts about herself.

Her soul experienced a holy disturbance and seemed fearful that what was taking place before her eyes might be an illusion of the senses or a snare laid by the spirit who tempts men.

The angel said to her: *"Blessed are you among women"* (Lk 1:28—Vulgate), but she regarded herself as the least of all and could not understand how such praise could be given her.

The angel also told her: *"You have found favor with God"* (Lk 1:30) and, if she consented, would become His Mother.

The thought of the sublime dignity reserved for her caused Mary to humble herself and regard herself as only too blessed if she might be God's servant.

If you yearn for glory, Mary teaches you where it is to be found. Glory that is authentic and solidly grounded consists in making yourself little.

That is the way God Himself thinks, for it is written: *He who is least among you is the greatest* (Lk 22:26).

That kind of greatness is solid and sure. No one will fight you for it or think of snatching it from you.

If you become the least, you will become the greatest. The conviction that you are and can do nothing will humble you and in that very act raise you up to the God Whom you acknowledge as sovereign source of all good.

You can then rely on the Divine power with all the more confidence as He finds His greatest delight in strengthening the weak.

Humility will free you from all the vileness into which ambition and pride lead men. What soul can be more base than that of the man who is ruled by pride and wants to be applauded at any cost?

Humility will free you from false respect for men and from the worthless ideas men have. You will be able to say with the Apostle: *"It matters little to me that you pass judgment on me. . . . I acknowledge but one judge, and that is God"* (1 Cor 4:3-5).

Humility will make you look with detachment at the world's honors, for behind the splendid facade lurk illusion and emptiness.

Humility will teach you not to vie with your neighbor but to honor him, and to have no envy when you see him raised above you, whether in rank or in esteem.

The natural man regards humility as base, because he judges entirely according to the senses and perceives only sensible things. Yet humility is one of the virtues best fitted to form great and noble hearts.

Of all the virtues, humility is the one that most steadies the spirit and most strengthens the soul.

Above all, it is the most beautiful element of likeness to Jesus, the God-man and source of true greatness and glory.

A man is never greater and more resplendent than when he devotes himself to imitating this divine model. Never do we draw closer to Him than when we are humble and love humiliation.

Jesus was humble and loved humiliation because He knew how much He thereby honored His Father.

It was when Jesus was undergoing humiliation that His heavenly Father declared: "*In Him I find My delight*" (Mt 3:17). It was then too that the angels sang: "*Glory to God in the highest*" (Lk 2:14).

If you become humble like Jesus, God will be glorified. Is there anything more splendid than to glorify God?

Prayer

Queen of heaven, in you the prophecy was luminously fulfilled: "*Whoever humbles himself shall be exalted*" (Mt 23:12); indeed you were all the more exalted because your humility was so great. Obtain for me the graces I need if I am to destroy the great pride that masters me.

Until now I have had but the outward marks of humility, practiced a false humility that I might win the world's esteem, for though the world corrupts all it touches, it nonetheless despises the proud.

Win for me a heartfelt humility that will keep me convinced of my weakness; a humility that will make me, like you, refer everything to God, expect all from Him, and depend on Him in everything; a humility that will win me the esteem of God Himself who is the only source of greatness and honor.

CHAPTER 14

THE HUMBLE SOUL TRIES TO CONCEAL FROM MEN ITS TRUE VALUE IN GOD'S EYES

THE angel whom the Lord sent to Mary bestowed on her the greatest possible praise and told her she was to become the Mother of God's Son. Yet for the time being she told no one else what the angel had said to her.

She did not claim to be the Mother of the Messiah nor act outwardly as the person thus chosen. On the contrary, she acted outwardly just like other women.

Though she loved her husband Joseph very deeply and spoke often with him, she did not tell him of what had happened.

When she went to visit Elizabeth, she found that the mystery was already known, but she did not therefore instruct her cousin more fully about the events.

Mary left it up to God to decide when the time was ripe for revealing a secret that would redound so greatly to His glory.

Her only concern was to remain humble.

Men must learn to hide from the eyes of other men their own true value in God's eyes and the gifts they have received from His generous hands.

A virtue that is hidden is always safe; it leaves it entirely up to God to manifest it as He will.

When a person shows his treasure for all to see, he risks losing it. Even the brightest colors are somewhat dulled by intense light.

Martha said to her sister: *"The Lord is here and is asking for you"* (Jn 11:28), but she whispered the message.

Men, being blind and sense-bound, *do not understand* and value what lies beyond the senses, that is, *what is proper to the Spirit of God* (1 Cor 2:14). To speak of it to them is to expose holy things to ridicule.

The Spirit of God communicates Himself in secret and desires that whatever goes on between Himself and the beloved soul should remain secret.

Only one human individual, chosen out of all the others, can and should be told of the spiritual riches you have received, so that he may instruct you and make the riches bear fruit. Here on earth he represents God in guiding you along the path of salvation and perfection.

In the eyes of all the rest be like other upright and virtuous men: humble, modest, affable, and even-tempered; but let your inner self be closed to them.

If they think that you have but little experience of spiritual things and are quite different from what you in fact are, this is all to the good, for it will enable you to keep hidden the graces God has bestowed on you.

God wants you to walk in His paths, but we are much better off if we walk noiselessly.

Some men have received very special favors from God but then have ruined themselves by concentrating too much on these favors, for they have become unjustifiably complacent and sought the admiration of those who should have never come to know of these favors.

If such men had had the interior disposition of the Blessed Virgin, that is, her spirit of humility, God would constantly have enlightened them, inspired a distrust of self, and taught them to see the tricks that self-love plays.

We must always be concerned with avoiding spiritual illusion, but this holds especially if we are walking an extraordinary path.

Profound virtue that is entirely Divine in origin and character can at times be changed into hateful vice, if we are not careful to avoid self-deception.

A truly interior soul always suffers and must draw on all its capacity for submission to God's will, when He allows some special grace He has given it to be outwardly manifested.

CHAPTER 15

THE PRUDENCE OF FAITH

MARY *considered* (Lk 1:29), says the Gospel, when the angel spoke to her on God's behalf. She reflected because she was humble and because her faith was deep.

This *Virgin most prudent* knew that the angel of darkness sometimes disguises himself as an angel of light and that the spirit of falsehood imitates at times the voice of the spirit of truth.

Therefore Mary questioned the angel and waited for his answer, so that she might judge whether it agreed with what the prophets had said about the Messiah and with the principles of her religion.

Thus, when the angel spoke, she needed no other guide for her action, for in his words she recognized the word of God.

Here we have a prudence which is controlled by the obedience of faith and is never contrary to faith.

Prudence opens a person's eyes so as to be sure that a revelation has been given, and submission to faith closes them so as to believe blindly.

Do not trust every spirit (1 Jn 4:1).

In all that concerns religion I must believe only what God has told me either directly or through the Church, which is *the pillar and bulwark of the truth* (1 Tim 3:15).

God has given us the means of knowing what He has revealed; once revelation is certain, then *accursed be even an angel* (Gal 1:8) if he suggests to me the contrary of what revelation teaches me.

I believe what my religion teaches me, for it teaches me nothing that God has not revealed. And what can be more certain than what I am told by Him Who is Truth itself?

It is not possible for God to deceive me or to be deceived.

It would be madness for me to accept something as God's word without sufficient reason for doing so; that has been the folly of the pagans and of many Christians too.

On the other hand, to accept something as God's word when I have good reasons for doing so is evidence of the highest wisdom.

To believe with unshakable faith the truth which God has revealed is to share in the infallibility of God Himself.

When we examine our religion in the spirit of Mary we become more firmly grounded in our faith.

Yet there are some who examine their religion with the purpose of gaining support for the errors they love and not of learning what they ought to believe and love.

Their purpose is not to discover and embrace the truth but to find, if possible, reasons for doubting truths they cannot bring themselves to admit.

Such people are not seeking sure norms for recognizing what they ought to believe and how they ought to live; their purpose is rather to continue in their guilty state without suffering remorse for it.

Many find faith too troublesome and gladly look for a system to justify their lack of religious spirit.

Faith becomes subject to doubt only when it becomes troublesome.

Unbelievers rebel at the holiness of its principles no less than at the incomprehensibility of its mysteries.

We must either mortify our own passions or suffer constant remorse and fear. In the second case, we will decide either to believe nothing at all or at least to doubt everything except the perverse state in which we will find ourselves.

CHAPTER 16

SUBMISSION TO FAITH

WHEN Mary was sure that God was indeed speaking to her through the angel's mouth, she firmly believed that He would accomplish all that the angel had foretold; she believed it without trying to understand it fully.

She did not ask for a miracle, as Ahaz did (cf. Isa 7); she did not doubt, as Zechariah did (cf. Lk 1); it was not at this moment of faith that she said: *"How can this be?"* (cf. Lk 1:34).

How would the Child, whose Mother she was to be, effect redemption? What would be the basis of His kingdom? The angel hears no such questions from her; he finds in her none of the curiosity that marks weaker souls. No: she immediately bends her mind under the yoke of faith.

Follow her example, my soul, and humble yourself! Bow your reason before truths beyond your power to comprehend.

Do not seek fully to understand the mysteries faith proposes to you. If you understood them fully, they would no longer be mysteries! It is enough for you to know that they are true.

But you cannot be convinced of their truth if you mistakenly think that faith teaches them in a way that will make them acceptable to everyone.

The mysteries, I admit, cannot be fully comprehended; but faith would cease to be meritorious if human reason could explain it.

"Blessed are those who have not seen and yet have come to believe!" (Jn 20:29). Every part of nature, from the distant stars to the tiniest flower, is a mystery to you. You admit you do not understand these natural mysteries. Do you expect then to understand the mysteries of God?

Do you expect to see clearly the things of God when you see so imperfectly those of earth?

We must not compare the weak powers of the human mind with the power and mighty works of a Being Who is infinitely beyond our understanding.

God would no longer be God if we were able to penetrate with our minds the depths of His being.

To believe what the eye does not see and reason does not comprehend is to offer perfect homage to the supreme truth.

My God, I want to judge things no longer by my own light but by the light faith gives me.

You ask of me not only the sacrifices of the heart but also that sacrifice of the mind which faith involves.

I hope some day to reach heaven where everything will be made clear to me. Yet even in heaven I shall never succeed in fully comprehending either Your perfections or Your works, for You will always be infinite and I will always be limited.

I believe, Lord! Strengthen my weak faith; increase my faith! (Mk 9:24).

You cannot deny me the gift of faith, if I ask it of You as I ought, for it is the source of all Your other gifts.

I ask that gift of You through the Blessed Virgin's intercession. For, because of her obedient and meritorious faith, she saw fulfilled in herself what You had foretold.

Grant me a living, all-embracing faith: a faith that is sure and makes no exceptions. To doubt is to fail to believe; to make an exception of a single article is to reject them all.

Grant me a faith that is enlivened by love, for it is love that will make me live according to the truths faith teaches me.

I do not ask You to work in me the miracles which faith worked in Your saints; I do ask You for the faith that made them saints.

CHAPTER 17

EAGERNESS TO RECEIVE JESUS IN COMMUNION

Mary

MY CHILD, the mystery on which you are meditating suggests thoughts beyond your imagining.

The Believer

Queen of heaven, please instruct me yourself. *Speak, Lord! Your servant is listening!* (1 Sam 3:19).

Mary

Before receiving the angel's visit I had often prayed, like the holy men of Israel, *"Drop down dew, you heavens, and let the clouds rain down the Just One"* (Isa 45:8). But I never dared think I might be the virgin who would give the world its Savior.

But when I was sure that I had been chosen to be His Mother, I humbled myself before such a lofty and sublime destiny and was filled with sentiments of intense love. What joy I felt at possessing God within my womb!

This same God Who in His incarnation deigned to unite Himself so closely to me also wants to be united to you, my child, through Communion. But you are much less eager to receive than He is to give.

Your laziness and a false humility will suggest excuses for staying away from the holy table; do not accept them.

There is the excuse of fear and reverence; but fear and reverence must be subordinated to love and simply serve to make love more attentive.

To stay away from Communion out of false reverence is to rob Jesus of the satisfaction He finds in dwelling with you.

He has told you of this satisfaction when He said: *"My delight is to be with the children of men"* (Prov 8:31).

You say that because of your frequent sins you dare not frequently approach the Holy of Holies. But, my child, however weak a soul may be, if it makes every effort to improve, Jesus will always find it a joy to come to it.

You say you stay away from Communion because you feel yourself unworthy. You ought rather to say: I want to try to become worthy, as far as I can, of receiving Communion, so that

I may share in the graces Jesus gives to devout souls who unite themselves to Him in Communion.

Your Communions are infrequent only because you fear the inconvenience they involve and the obligations they impose.

You are afraid of the fervent life that is required if you are to receive Communion frequently.

You bemoan your soul's weakness and frailty. Well, then, profit by the effective remedy offered you in the *bread of life* (Jn 6:35).

In His Gospel Jesus calls to the divine banquet *the poor and the crippled, the blind and the lame* (Lk 14:21).

He is well aware of your wretched state and therefore in His sacrament offers you a food that strengthens and gives courage.

It would be best, of course, if you brought to Communion a perfect holiness; but Jesus does not require that.

In fact, if perfect holiness were required, few indeed would be admitted to His table, despite all His invitations!

To claim that such holiness is required for communicating is to turn the fruit of Communion into a disposition for Communion.

Therefore, bring to Communion a sincere sense of your own unworthiness; most especially, bring a great purity of heart or at least a firm determination that you will try to reach such purity. Then your Communion will be what it ought to be.

Remember that Communion properly received never fails to profit a soul.

If you are watchful and faithful and thus maintain the dispositions that will allow you to receive Communion frequently, you will be already well advanced along the path of perfection.

The soul that is impatient to enjoy the presence of Jesus in heaven will find its delight in enjoying that presence on earth through the frequent reception of Communion.

CHAPTER 18

SENTIMENTS AFTER COMMUNION

Mary

MY CHILD, when you have received Jesus at the holy table and He now rests within your heart, make your own the sentiments that were mine as I carried Him in my womb.

The Believer

Mary, no human mind can conceive, no tongue express the sentiments and emotions of your heart at that time. God alone knows them!

Faith, humility, zeal, gratitude, love, and all the other virtues filled every moment of the nine months during which the Word of God dwelled in your holy womb.

Mary

My child, if you knew the value of the gift Jesus gives you in giving Himself to you in Communion and the sentiments toward you which fill His soul, would you lack the proper sentiments toward Him?

Here the creature is visited by the Creator; a beggar by the King of glory; an afflicted soul by the heavenly consoler; a man who is all sin by Him Who is holiness itself.

Humble yourself profoundly before Him; praise His goodness which is infinitely greater than anything you can imagine.

Loathe your own past ingratitude; ask His help for the future; promise Him undying fidelity.

Abandon yourself to the impulses of purest joy. Ask the angels and saints to offer Jesus thanks on your behalf, thanks that are adequate, if that be possible, to the splendid gift He gives you.

Desire that a God so good and lovable be loved and glorified on earth as He is in heaven.

Open your heart to His blazing love and desire to be consumed by it.

In gratitude for His blessings and to make up for your own weakness, offer Him all the sentiments which have filled holy souls as they received Him with devoted love in this sacrament.

Offer Him especially the sentiments with which He deigned to fill my soul when in His incarnation He united Himself so closely to me.

Think of the power of which He offers you so marvelous an example in the Eucharist; think especially of His humility and ask Him for the grace to imitate it.

In this sacrament His humanity as well as His Divinity is hidden. Nothing of Jesus is visible, except to the eyes of your faith.

Ask Him that you may love a life that is hidden and despised; that you may flee from outward show and honors; that you may do all you do without any desire to be seen and esteemed.

In this sacrament Jesus is treated with contempt by many, and with indifference by many others who are little concerned with Him, much with the world, and entirely with themselves. Ask for the grace to bear patiently with insults and opposition.

Such, my child, are the thoughts that ought to fill you at Communion time and throughout any day on which you have been privileged to receive Jesus.

CHAPTER 19

DRYNESS OF SOME SOULS IN THE PRACTICE OF PIETY AND EVEN IN COMMUNION

The Believer

MARY, next to Jesus you are my refuge and my counselor. Thank you for the instruction you have so kindly given me.

Yet, holy Virgin, at Communion time, despite my efforts to have the sentiments which the presence of the Body and Blood of the Lord should inspire in me, my soul is often dry, my heart cold.

Why is it that I cannot share at that time in the sentiments of tender love and sensible sweetness that must have been yours when you carried Jesus in your womb and which devout souls share when they receive Communion?

Mary

My child, when you find yourself dry at Communion time, humble yourself with the reflection that you deserve such a condition because of your unfaithfulness. Then bear your burden patiently in expiation of your sins and do not lose heart.

If you have reason to believe that your state of deprivation is really a punishment, then change your ways. If it is only a trial, then turn it into a source of merit through your submission.

The profit from a good Communion is not necessarily connected with enjoyment at the time of reception. The profit to which I refer is fidelity to one's duties.

A heart may be sincerely and entirely dedicated to God and yet find no pleasure in the things of God.

Many souls who are advancing fervently along the path of perfection are tested by dryness in prayer and even when they approach the Eucharistic table.

Virtue does not depend on tangible consolation. On the contrary, it is to be feared that souls may not be sufficiently detached from such consolation.

The Divine Spouse knows quite well what souls need. He gives to some a sweetness and consolation He does not give to others, because He wants the latter to adore without seeking to understand fully.

A negligent soul must not expect generosity on the part of Jesus. On the other hand, a faithful and fervent person ought not to regret having occasion to show Jesus that he serves Him for His own sake than for His gifts.

Do not think, then, that God is rejecting you when you feel repugnance in His service. Instead strive faithfully to please Him, and do all as though you found His service delightful.

My child, go to your God through faith rather than through the senses. Try to please Him in all things. If you succeed, you will have found the happiness the saints sought and found.

The state of dryness can be a great help to holiness if you profit by it to adapt yourself to the divine plan.

What God intends to accomplish through your persevering in such a state is to teach you not to seek yourself but to find your happiness and merit in pleasing Him.

The Believer

Holy Virgin, I deserve no consolation, and in this as in all things I bow to the will of the Divine Teacher.

Blessed be He if in His mercy He places me among those to whom He grants these sensible consolations. But blessed be He, too, if He denies me them.

I ask no other consolation of Jesus than to be faithful to Him.

I regard myself as infinitely blessed if I may sacrifice all my own heart's desires to those of the Heart of Jesus, my God, and if I may do my duty without having any other pleasure than that of knowing that I do it in order to please Him.

CHAPTER 20

FRUIT TO BE DERIVED FROM COMMUNION FOR THE CONDUCT OF OUR LIVES

The Believer

MOTHER OF PURE LOVE (Sir 24:24), you were entirely holy from the first moment of your existence; yet, once the Word had taken flesh in your chaste womb, what new progress you made in holiness! The presence of Jesus within you for nine months left in you impulses to holiness that would last all your life.

The thought of the extraordinary favor God had bestowed on you kept alive in you to your last breath a holy concern for finding the means, and profiting by all the occasions, of expressing your gratitude to Him.

Mary

My child, my example indeed ought to put you to shame. You receive in Communion the all-holy God, yet you yourself are far from holy.

A single Communion should be enough to fill you with all the fervor of the saints, yet all your Communions leave you as cold as you were before.

You are always to some degree reserved in dealing with Jesus, though He does not hold back at all in heaping His blessings upon you.

His presence when you have received Him indeed inspires in you great desires of virtue, and you promise Him much. But the desires and the promises soon fade.

You would certainly not deal in this way with an important man of this world if he honored you with a visit.

How aware you are of the gifts a friend gives you! How ready to thank him! Love cannot rest until it has found a way of expressing its gratitude.

Can it be, my child, that you lack occasions for practicing virtue, such as the saints made use of after Communion when they wanted to show Jesus how sensible they were of the graces they had received?

What He asks for more than anything else is that you keep careful watch over your affections so that they are all directed to Him.

If you were to keep careful watch over yourself after receiving Communion, you would retain the devotion you had at the time of Communion.

Such watchfulness after every Communion is the best means you have of preparing for the next.

The Believer

Virgin, model of every virtue, I kneel at your feet, filled with shame at my coldness and ingratitude.

Pray to Jesus for me that He will never come to my heart without directing all its movements and turning them entirely to Himself.

May He take away this wretched heart of mine that is so unworthy of Him and create in me a new heart. May He give me a heart like yours: ardent and generous, tender and constant toward Him, as yours now is toward us.

CHAPTER 21

LOVE OF NEIGHBOR

The Believer

NOT without good reason, most fervent Virgin, did you leave the solitude of Nazareth and come before the eyes of men. The spirit of love inspired you.

Fortunate the hills that felt your footsteps! Mountains of Judea, exult at the glory that was yours!

Worthy Mother of the God of love, hardly had the angel told you of your holy cousin Elizabeth's condition when you hurried off to visit her.

She *went in haste* (Lk 1:39), says the Gospel. The inspirations of the Spirit must be promptly carried out.

The mountains you had to cross did not make you hesitate even for a moment. Love does its duty with courage and generosity.

You left behind for a while the sweet pleasures of your retreat, for love has its rights and the consolations of devotion must yield to them.

Your love was not simply a thing of the passing moment: you *stayed about three months* (Lk 1:56) with Elizabeth and lavished care and attention upon her.

What happy effects of holiness this loving visit produced! Elizabeth was filled with the Holy Spirit and John the Baptist was sanctified in his mother's womb.

Elizabeth and her husband were already living virtuous lives, but your example taught them a still more perfect love.

Mary

My child, if you love the Lord, you will also love your neighbor for whose sake He came down from heaven, became a man, and offered His own life on the Cross.

Do not be satisfied with sentiments; let your love take concrete form. Many who are afflicted need the comfort of your words; many who are unhappy need the help of your generous gifts.

God has allowed many people to be unhappy in this world so that they might achieve holiness through their suffering and you through your charity.

Be ready to give all the help you can. Delay always means the loss of some of love's merit.

Let your love be generous and extend as far as possible.

To limit the service you offer your neighbor is to evade rather than carry out the duties of love.

When you yourself cannot help your neighbor, then try to bring others to help him, or at least invoke the Lord's providential care over him.

See in your neighbor not a mere man but God Himself. Then, no matter who asks your help, you will refuse him nothing, because you do not want to refuse it to the Lord.

If you do good to men because they deserve it and are good men, you will do it but rarely.

My child, prefer those works of love which are costly and be charitable at the expense of your self-love.

God Himself teaches us by His example to do good to all men, even to the most ungrateful.

"Give," says Jesus, *"and it shall be given to you"* (Lk 6:38). Give every temporal good, and God will give you eternal goods in their place.

Give your neighbor your good advice, so that he may emerge from his uncertainty. Then your God will inspire you and help you out of your own perplexities.

Give the afflicted a consoling word. Then *the God of all consolation* (2 Cor 1:3) will sustain you in your own afflictions by His powerful grace.

CHAPTER 22

THE GREATNESS OF GOD

MY SOUL, listen to Mary as under the holy impulse of love she praises the greatness of her God.

Make your own the sentiments that fill her heart; unite your praises to hers.

Together with her glorify the Lord God Almighty Who when He pleases works the greatest wonders and Whose infinitely holy name deserves praise from all the world. He is *the God Who shows might with His arm in order to pull down the powerful and raise up the humble and Who despoils the rich in order to heap blessings on the poor* (Lk 1:47-53).

And indeed, to whom are glory and praise really due if not to You, my God?

The greatness of men is limited, brittle, and artificial; it depends on our estimates of things and is often false and purely imaginary.

Your glory, however, my God, is unlimited. You possess it by Your very being, and every other greatness must bow down to Yours.

The greatness of kings ends with their death. The news of their fall is followed straightway by everlasting oblivion.

But You, Lord, exist forever. Your glory cannot be limited to the boundaries of the universe or time.

For what can Your creatures glorify themselves? From You, after all, comes all their power and wealth. They can do naught without Your aid; You can do whatever You want independently of them.

You alone are great of Your very self. You need no power from outside in order to accomplish what You desire.

To will and to do are one and the same thing for You.

Without going outside Yourself, You find in Yourself in an absolutely unlimited and perfect form whatever perfections other beings, visible and invisible, may possess.

You alone possess in Your very nature all possible perfections, for You alone possess all being in its fullness.

The great men of this world do not deserve our homage unless they reflect Your greatness in themselves because You have deigned to communicate to them a share in Your own power. And even then, what are they in Your sight but *dust and ashes* (Job 42:6), like all other men?

All human greatness, therefore, is overshadowed when set before You, and vanishes away.

There is no true greatness except for that which can be neither increased nor diminished.

Prayer

Lord, God of the heavenly powers, what can be compared with You? You alone deserve the adoration of heaven and earth, for You alone are great, always great, great in everything that exists. You are great in all Your works, in the smallest no less than in the most striking, in the flowers of the field no less than in the stars of heaven. You are great in wisdom, power, justice, and goodness. Our great God, who can ever speak worthily of Your greatness?

I admit my own inability to praise You, even as I proclaim Your glory. I render my homage to Your infinite greatness, even as I acknowledge that greatness to be greater than any words can express.

CHAPTER 23

GOD'S MERCY

MARY, how I would like to have heard you praise the Lord's mercies as well as His great deeds! What sublime thoughts would then fill my heart!

As I review with you the long series of those who from generation to generation have feared the Lord, I find no one who was not overwhelmed by His mercy.

If in His anger He strikes sinners and tries them with great chastisements, He does so only after having attempted through blessings to make them come to their senses and turn their affections to Him.

The ingratitude and infidelity of His people could not dry up the well of His goodness. Instead, with tender paternal love He continued to throw open to them the treasures of His mercy.

He had promised Abraham and his descendants forever (Lk 1:55) that He would send a rescuer, and, rather than betray His promises, He tried to find in the fathers reasons for giving their sons the graces of which they had proved unworthy.

The Rescuer came and men could not fail to see the immense love God had for them.

He had held out His helping hand to all who were unhappy; sinners, far from being excluded from His blessings, were even the chief object of His zeal.

It was with sorrow that He saw Himself abandoned by so many ingrates who preferred an illusory freedom to the priceless blessing of being counted among His servants and friends.

As crowning proof of His inexhaustible love He mounted the Cross and there shed His own blood to the last drop.

Men saw Him in this condition and see Him still, yet their hearts are not touched. Nonetheless the lightning that should annihilate them has not yet been hurled. His mercy and the plea uttered by His blood are still to be heard interceding for them.

Holy Virgin, I myself am evident proof of His patience in waiting for the sinner and of the tender reception He gives him.

I was a sheep gone astray and the Divine Shepherd led me back to the fold. In His mercy He carried me Himself for fear I would be too weak to return under my own power.

Can I forget the day when this loving Father, seeing His prodigal son returning, embraced me, bathed me in His tears, and clasped me to His breast?

How good this God is Who, when He sees *a contrite and humbled heart* (Ps 51:19), forgets that He is a judge and remembers only that He is a father!

Prayer

Virgin Mother of the God *of mercies* (2 Cor 1:3) you prayed for my conversion. Win for me now the grace to persevere!

You know how inconstant I am in desiring what is best. Protect me now and preserve, strengthen, and perfect in me the new longing for holiness that grace has inspired in me.

Your love for me will surely not be less than the confidence I have in you.

Shall the enemy of my salvation do more to destroy me than you will do to save me?

Most compassionate and lovable of all mothers, be merciful and obtain for me from your Son a lively dissatisfaction with the past, a scrupulous fidelity in my present life, and an unshakable trust for the future. *Then I will sing forever in heaven the mercies of the Lord and your goodness* (Ps 89:2).

CHAPTER 24

**GRATITUDE TO GOD
FOR HIS BLESSINGS**

Prayer

GOD, infinitely good, till now You have given me so many blessings both temporal and spiritual. In thanksgiving I offer You all the sentiments of gratitude which Mary felt throughout her life as she reflected on Your gifts, but especially those she expressed when she entered the home of Zechariah and Elizabeth.

Elizabeth praised Mary as she deserved. But Mary wanted Elizabeth to forget the recipient of God's blessings and to think only of the Giver.

Mary would have liked to unite herself to every creature in order to praise You, my God, and thank You for the favors You had given her.

She regarded herself as happy only because *He who is mighty has deigned to look upon His servant in her lowliness and to show how great and merciful He is* (Lk 1:47-50).

How lacking I am, Lord, in such sentiments as these, even though You have given me so many proofs of Your love! I am naught but an ungrateful man.

I receive blessings from You and I thank men for them! My plans turn out well and I attribute the success to my own efforts.

Most of all, what am I and what can I do with regard to my own salvation? Yet I do not think of thanking You for the great helps You have given me so that I may succeed in this all-important undertaking.

If in any way I am pleasing in Your sight, it is due to You alone, and without You I cannot continue to please You.

What a wretched and weak man I am! If Your grace were to desert me, Lord, what would become of me? Into what dreadful corruption would not my evil inclinations lead me?

There is no security for me except in the conviction of my own weakness and in gratitude for the graces with which You mercifully sustain me.

My God, do not let my infidelity make me unworthy of Your gifts or ingratitude make me forget them.

The great desire of Your heart is to do good. But I know too that ingratitude is the fault that may most easily turn aside Your mercies from me.

So often I have deserved to experience no longer the effects of Your mercy, but You have determined to win my heart over by Your gifts.

My great God, I will resist You no longer! Henceforth I shall dedicate myself entirely to You. And as I live only by Your grace, so too I want to live only for You.

Be gracious to me and grant that, as my needs and Your gifts are endless, I may also pass my life in unbroken prayer for Your generosity and in gratitude for Your blessings.

CHAPTER 25

VISITS

MARY'S example in the visit she paid her cousin Elizabeth should guide my conduct in social relationships.

This humble Virgin was Mother of God, yet she did not wait for Elizabeth to visit her. Her conduct is a condemnation of the distorted sensitivity of those many people who are jealous of their status and fight tooth and nail for the precedence they think they deserve.

But what was Mary's reason for visiting her cousin? Piety, and nothing else.

Yet curiosity, vanity, and self-love are the motives for most of the visits men pay each other in our world.

Such was not the visit paid by the faithful Virgin. Her reasons were entirely holy.

Virtuous people act under the influence of virtue even in the visits they pay, dictated though these may seem to be by simple good manners.

Piety, love, and the glory of God guided Mary's steps. She entered a home where He was loved and served. She came to congratulate her relative on the graces which God had given her and of which the angel had informed Mary. She came on a visit in order to be of help and to strengthen the bonds of holy friendship.

Piety does not stand in the way of fulfilling the duties of social life; it does, however, sanctify the latter by steeping them in Christian spirit.

The Christian tries to draw profit from every moment. Therefore, he tries also, as far as possible, to break off useless relationships and visits that have only pleasure as their motive.

Devout people like to pay visits that serve for mutual edification and have no use for any others.

Virtue likes to find itself in touch with virtue. All other visits prove wearisome, for devout people suffer when outside the atmosphere that sustains them.

The saints press even the most unlikely actions into the service of God's glory, the neighbor's edification, and their own perfection.

If we were to imitate them and were inspired by the same spirit in the visits we pay each other, how profitable we would find these social relations which form part of our duties as members of society! We would enjoy countless innocent pleasures unknown to men of the world; we would inspire each other to virtue; we would end our visits, not with the empty feeling left by the tedious visits men of the world pay each other, but with the holy joy which is the heritage of upright men.

Christian souls, keep constantly before you the model I have offered you. Like Mary, leave your solitude only infrequently and deal only with virtuous men.

Like Mary, seek only to glorify God and edify your neighbor. Then you will profit by the relations you must maintain with men.

CHAPTER 26

CONVERSATIONS

IN imagination I enter Elizabeth's home as Mary came to visit her.

What lessons of modesty, humility, discretion, and love I learn here!

Elizabeth recognized Mary as Mother of her God (cf. Lk 1:42-43), showered gifts and blessings upon her, praised her greatness, and congratulated her on the extraordinary favors God had done her.

Far from letting herself be dazzled by her own dignity, Mary gave back to God the praise offered her and used the occasion to glorify the Lord.

She admitted that *God Who is mighty has done great things for me* (Lk 1:49) but she also assigned all the glory to Him. She did not forget that, though she was Mother of God, she was also *the servant of the Lord* (Lk 1:38). Here is sincere humility with none of that false modesty that so often masks a secret pride.

How many people refuse the praise offered them because they hope thereby to win even greater praise! Thus they press modesty itself into the service of vanity.

Mary and Elizabeth thought only of God and His great deeds and mercies. They were filled with love and found their delight in telling of the wonderful things His wisdom, power, and goodness had accomplished.

The mouth speaks whatever fills the heart (Mt 12:34). You speak only of the world and its empty show; that is sure proof that you love only the world and that your heart is the victim of its illusions.

"*Those others belong to the world,*" said Jesus to His beloved disciple; "*that is why what they say is from the world, and the world listens to them*" (1 Jn 4:5). If they belonged to God they would speak of Him or at least say nothing that was not inspired by His spirit.

Remember that when God judges you, *you will have to render an account for every word* (Mt 12:36). What a good reason for you to be afraid!

How few conversations take place even among professedly devout people that do not lengthen the account we must render to God!

What can they find to talk about so much? Frivolous matters, rumors, worthless things. Even the conversations they regard as most innocent are of that kind.

It seems, moreover, that they cannot converse without speaking of the defects of their neighbors. Conversation languishes when it stops being critical or even malicious.

Woe to you, malicious tongues! With serpent's fangs you delight to destroy the reputations of the absent! Woe to those who enjoy hearing such talk! Anyone who freely listens to evil talk shares the blame for it.

CHAPTER 27

TRUE FRIENDSHIP

The Believer

A FAITHFUL friend, says Scripture, *is a rich treasure. That gift is given only to those who fear the Lord* (Sir 6:14, 17).

Mary, God enabled you to find that priceless treasure in Elizabeth, and she found it in you.

Each of you provides a model of perfect friendship, of holy friendship that was free of all that corrupts human friendships.

A happy similarity of sentiments—religious sentiments—linked you together. Grace and virtue were the gifts you valued in Elizabeth and the gifts she valued in you.

You spoke frequently to each other, confided in each other, offered each other advice, and competed in serving each other. But all the proofs of friendship which you offered each other had a single ultimate purpose: the glorification of God.

Elizabeth must have seen that, after she had become united in spirit to you, her relationship to God was deeper than before.

You, holy Virgin, made the same progress in holiness while in your cousin's house that you would have made in the solitude of Nazareth.

You were content with the union between you and broke off your visit without ceasing to love each other. The virtue that unites two hearts cannot fall victim to inconstancy.

Mary

Do not deceive yourself, my child; you will not taste the innocent delights of friendship unless you seek them in a holy friendship.

In choosing friends people often make mistakes. You should give your confidence only to those you know to be faithful and on whose religious spirit you can rely.

Make it a matter of conscience never to speak evil of anyone. If you cannot prevent others from backbiting, at least let them know by your silence that you accept no part of their malicious gossip.

Shrink from any talk that is not decent. Do not smile at the talk the world calls good-humored, but which is really indecent.

Take pride, above all, in being regarded as a person in whose presence people dare not attack religion and piety. Reproach the wicked man with a holy freedom, and if you have no other way of checking his evil tongue, at least show your disapproval by stern silence.

Be truthful in what you say, modest and prudent in your words. Be affable to all, take part in innocent joys. Virtue allows that and at times even orders it.

The more you are exposed to the danger of sinning with your tongue, the greater caution you should show in forcing it to silence.

If you love being alone with God in your house, you will be able to handle yourself better when you have to go out among men.

Before entering into conversation ask the Lord: *Set a guard over my mouth, O Lord, keep watch over the door of my lips* (Ps 141:3); then reflect that He is present and listening to you. Speak to Him interiorly from time to time with sentiments of love.

When a conversation is finished reflect on the words you have spoken. Thank God if you have acted properly. Discipline yourself for faults you have committed.

If you follow these rules you will attain that discretion and wise reserve which the masters of the spiritual life so strongly urge and which they rightly regard as a matter of high perfection.

You will find many ordinary friends who will offer you outward signs of affection, but you expect nothing more from them.

Such people will be your friends as long as they can profit by your prosperity. They will suddenly stop being your friends if your fortunes take a turn for the worse.

They will try to correct those defects in you which may cause harm to themselves, but they are unconcerned with defects which Christianity struggles against and the world cherishes.

Be aware, then, of what makes a true friend: help in need, comfort in affliction, light in uncertainty, counsel in affairs, guidance back to the straight path when you have gone astray, and, above all, exhortation, by word and example, to the carrying out of your duties. But such friends are rarely found, because it is rare that in choosing friends men take virtue into account.

Love virtue yourself, and you will surely find a worthy friend, another self.

Many friendships seem in the beginning to be sincere and deep, but they soon fade because faults are the only common bond.

As far as possible, make your friendship a source of edification; give your friends good example and receive good example from them. Find in such friendships all the delight your conscience will allow; but do not carry the delight too far.

Do not demand too much of your friends; avoid flattering them; above all, do not flatter them so that you may be flattered in turn!

CHAPTER 28

CONFIDENCE IN GOD AND ABANDONMENT TO HIS PROVIDENCE

TRUST in God is one of the greatest homages we can pay to His perfections. The greater our confidence, the more it honors Him. By it we acknowledge Him to be the supreme Being Who can do all that He wills. Confidence is one of the most effective means of winning many graces and special favors.

Mary gave us splendid proof of her own great confidence in God.

She left it to Him to take care of her reputation.

The husband given her as protector of her virginity felt anxious doubt arising in his heart and thought of abandoning her.

Yet Mary showed no uneasiness. She was full of confidence in God and humbly waited for the moment chosen by His providence. That moment did come. Joseph was enlightened by

STATIONS
of the
CROSS

1. Jesus is Condemned to Death
O Jesus, help me to appreciate Your sanctifying grace more and more.

2. Jesus Bears His Cross
O Jesus, You chose to die for me. Help me to love You always with all my heart.

3. Jesus Falls the First Time
O Jesus, make me strong to conquer my wicked passions, and to rise quickly from sin.

4. Jesus Meets His Mother
O Jesus, grant me a tender love for Your Mother, who offered You for love of me.

STATIONS
of the
CROSS

5. Jesus is Helped by Simon

O Jesus, like Simon lead me ever closer to You through my daily crosses and trials.

6. Jesus and Veronica

O Jesus, imprint Your image on my heart that I may be faithful to You all my life.

7. Jesus Falls a Second Time

O Jesus, I repent for having offended You. Grant me forgiveness of all my sins.

8. Jesus Speaks to the Women

O Jesus, grant me tears of compassion for Your sufferings and of sorrow for my sins.

STATIONS
of the
CROSS

9. Jesus Falls a Third Time

O Jesus, let me never yield to despair. Let me come to You in hardship and spiritual distress.

10. He is Stripped of His Garments

O Jesus, let me sacrifice all my attachments rather than imperil the divine life of my soul.

11. Jesus is Nailed to the Cross

O Jesus, strengthen my faith and increase my love for You. Help me to accept my crosses.

12. Jesus Dies on the Cross

O Jesus, I thank You for making me a child of God. Help me to forgive others.

STATIONS
of the
CROSS

13. Jesus is Taken down from the Cross

O Jesus, through the intercession of Your holy Mother, let me be pleasing to You.

14. Jesus is Laid in the Tomb

O Jesus, strengthen my will to live for You on earth and bring me to eternal bliss in heaven.

Prayer after the Stations

JESUS, You became an example of humility, obedience and patience, and preceded me on the way of life bearing Your Cross. Grant that, inflamed with Your love, I may cheerfully take upon myself the sweet yoke of Your Gospel together with the mortification of the Cross and follow You as a true disciple so that I may be united with You in heaven. Amen.

an angel through a dream and his doubt vanished. Full of reverence for the virtue of his wife, he did not hesitate to enter into a permanent union with her.

Here we can see how useful it is to trust in God and leave our interests in His care.

Everything is promised to the man who trusts: the dew of heaven and the fruitfulness of earth, the blessings of time and the blessings of eternity.

He who trusts in the strength of men will be like the grass that grows in the desert: its lot will be to wither away (cf. 1 Pet 1:24). But he who trusts in the Lord and relies on Him *is like a tree planted near streams of water, which bears fruit in its season, and whose leaves never wither. Everything he does will prosper* (Ps 1:3).

Everything urges us to confidence: God's goodness, His power, His promises, His fidelity, His knowledge of our needs, our own weakness, and our daily experience of the powerlessness and treachery of men.

Therefore rely trustingly on His providence in all your afflictions, no matter what they be. You complain that God does not help you in your trials. But before He sends help He wants your confidence to bring you to His feet in prayer for that help!

He undoubtedly does know your sorry state, but if your trust does not make you appeal to Him, He acts as though He did not know.

You get discouraged as though *there were no God in Israel* (2 Ki 1:6). Men are often upset, agitated, and disturbed when a single act of confidence would restore them to peace and calm.

In dangers, doubts, and anxieties seek counsel and comfort and try to alleviate your difficulties; but let God be your first source of help.

Men have no power, light, or will to help you except what has been given them by God.

As long as your trust in God does not become presumptuous, it can never be excessive. However weak a man may be of himself, he becomes strong through the action of God in Whom he trusts.

The events that have robbed you of your health have certainly not lessened the power of Him Who alone can restore that health to you.

If death has taken away someone on whom you relied, it has certainly not deprived you of Him Who guided that person in all that he did on your behalf.

If we reflect we will realize that God's help is not lessened except when our lack of confidence makes us unworthy of it.

CHAPTER 29

OBEDIENCE

MARY and Joseph, both of the Davidic line, went to Bethlehem to be enrolled in accordance with the edict of the emperor Augustus. The latter wanted to know the extent of his power and therefore ordered a census to be taken throughout the empire.

The holy pair did not reflect that in issuing his order the emperor was motivated by ambition and self-interest. No: they learned of the command and immediately obeyed.

If Augustus had known Mary perhaps he would have said, as Ahasuerus said to Esther: *"This decree was not meant for you"* (cf. Est 4:11). But he did not know her and included her under the edict just like everyone else. She obeyed like everyone else, and better than everyone else, because she obeyed humbly, patiently, and without murmuring.

She saw in the emperor's order the will of God. The order was, in her eyes, an act of Divine Providence and she submitted without questioning.

Obedience does not argue; simplicity is its hallmark. There is nothing more opposed to the spirit of submissiveness than the worldly prudence that wants to see and examine everything.

What would become of subordination if the orders of those who have the right to command were subjected to review by those whose duty it is to obey? If an earthly superior gives you a command, he does not merit your obedience because of any quality in himself; it is the supreme authority whom he represents that merits your obedience.

He who commands you can, admittedly, make mistakes, but as long as he commands nothing contrary to Divine Law, the obedience you give him and to God through him cannot be in error and is always greatly meritorious before God.

The saints teach us that it is more profitable to do small things under obedience than to do great things of one's own will.

Our modern-day wisdom scorns the simplicity of obedient hearts because it understands nothing of the things of God.

But what does the judgment of men matter to a person who takes the Gospel as the criterion of his judgments?

Obedience is not meritorious if it is given because of the good qualities of the person who commands. In that case the obedience is purely natural and you can expect no reward except from men.

Frequently, even in obedience rendered to God, men act so defectively and imperfectly that the obedience loses much of its value and merit.

If you do not obey promptly and joyously, except when the command accords with your own inclinations, you do your own will rather than the will of others.

The truly obedient man does not delay in carrying out commands nor does he grumble against the authority of superiors.

Sacred Scripture teaches us to submit respectfully to our superiors: not only to the good ones who act with moderation but also to those of difficult temperament.

You would find obedience difficult if you fastened your attention not on the man you are obeying but on God for Whose sake you ought to obey.

Victory is assured to the man who obeys (Prov 21:28), we are told by the Holy Spirit.

Self-will is a source of corruption. Obedience, when sanctified by a right intention, will enable us to avoid many evils and will win us God's approval.

MARRIAGE OF MARY AND JOSEPH

When Mary was about sixteen years old, she married a young carpenter named Joseph. They both took a vow of virginity in the married state.

BOOK 2

Life and Virtues of the Blessed Virgin Mary from the Birth of Her Divine Son, Jesus, to His Death

CHAPTER 1

BLESSED ARE THE POOR IN SPIRIT

The Believer

HOLY Virgin, I love to think of the deep peace that filled your soul in the stable at Bethlehem where Jesus was born.

Even the scornful refusals you met with as you sought for lodging could not lessen that peace.

The Queen of the angels was glad to be surrounded by poor shepherds, and the Mother of the Lord of time felt glad that she was left in a stable to face the severe weather of that harsh time of year. In that stable, Mary, you were infinitely more content with your great poverty than the rich of Bethlehem were with their wealth.

Mary

My child, learn from my example to set little store by earthly possessions and, if you are without them, to love the deprivation.

Can the poor really think of themselves as unfortunate when they see Jesus determining that His Mother too should be poor?

Can they think it when they see that He Himself at His birth had a poor rough manger for His cradle? When they consider that throughout His life Jesus had *nowhere to lay His head* (Mt 8:20) and that His deathbed was a cross?

The rich despise the poor. But God Himself says: *"Woe to you who are rich"* (Lk 6:24), and He invites the poor to His supper (cf. Lk 14:21).

Blessed are the poor in spirit, for theirs is the kingdom of heaven (Mt 5:3). These words refer to the poor who love their poverty and to the rich who are not attached to their wealth.

If a poor man were to reflect carefully on the holiness of his condition, he would certainly not set his heart on the wealth that could destroy him.

My child, when a man is prosperous he becomes attached to the things of earth and forgets heaven. Temptations become stronger and falls more frequent. To want riches is to want what is harmful to the soul.

There is no point to spending our lives accumulating earthly possessions, for we cannot take them with us when we die. The only thing we keep in death is virtue; the condition of poverty offers many occasions for exercising such virtue.

The Gospel tells us of a rich man who was *buried in hell*, whereas when Lazarus died, that poor man whom the rich man had scorned, *he was carried by angels to the bosom of Abraham* (Lk 16:22).

The Believer

You teach me, holy Virgin, that poverty is better than wealth. Teach me also henceforth to set my heart on heavenly possessions and to have a holy contempt for those of earth.

Chapter 2

VOLUNTARY POVERTY

The Believer

VIRGIN Mother of God, what great suffering poverty brought you! Yet you never complained and no one thought of relieving that poverty.

But why did you never point out to Jesus the harshness of your state? As Mother of God you had only to speak of it, and your Son could not have refused to change it. You would immediately have had all the angels at your service and they would have thought it a great honor to give you all the help you needed.

Mary

My child, if you possess Jesus, you are rich enough. A soul that considers God its sole blessing is indifferent toward earthly possessions and is quite willing to be poor.

When I saw that Jesus, king of heaven and earth, *though rich became poor so that He might enrich men by His poverty* (2 Cor 8:9), I made it my goal to imitate Him.

Blessed are those who are content to be poor or who strip themselves of this world's goods so that they may concentrate entirely on acquiring the riches of His love and the blessings of heaven! Blessed they who in imitation of Jesus gladly suffer the effects of poverty and are entirely detached from the things whose use they have!

Yet many of those who have embraced this state of perfection are far from the perfection their state requires of them! Their hearts are sometimes as attached to the little things they have been able to acquire as they would be to far greater possessions if they had them.

Can they be said to have made themselves poor for Jesus' sake when they only want the ease that wealth brings without having its inconveniences?

Jesus, born at Bethlehem, living at Nazareth, and dying on Calvary, is the model of those who for love of Him are content to be poor. He is also the model every Christian must try to imitate by being detached in heart and spirit from all riches.

The Holy Spirit does not tell everyone: "Give away all that you have." He does not require that degree of perfection from everyone, but He does say to everyone: "Do not be attached to possessions."

God cannot establish His rule in a heart that is attached to the passing things of earth.

Yet even if Jesus, on coming into this world, had not decided on a condition the world regards as unfortunate and if He had not scorned riches, we would nonetheless have to say that they are to be scorned.

For earthly possessions are deceitful and harmful, except for those who use them as a way of acquiring eternal possessions.

CHAPTER 3

LOVE FOR THE POOR

Mary

MY CHILD, love the poor. Be happy to use all the means you have of comforting them in their trials. If you do, you will prove yourself a true child of God who, as His holy scriptures tell us, expressly makes Himself the defender of the poor. He did not simply urge almsgiving but made it an obligation for all who are in a position to do it.

The Believer

Your own example, holy Virgin, supports your instruction. One of your greatest servants claims that you gave away to the poor the costly gifts the Savior had received from the Magi.

You preferred it to all the others you might have had for yourself. You wanted to remain in the need and obscurity into which the Lord determined you should be born, even though you were of David's line. What an example of detachment and love that you should give away to the poor what you might have used to alleviate your own poverty!

Mary

My child, the best use you can make of your abundance is to help the poor with it. If you do possess wealth, bear in mind that in giving it to you Divine Providence made you its administrator with a view to those who have no riches. Do not imitate the rich miser who always closes his heart to the needs of his brothers and would rather see them die a wretched death than deprive himself of something in order to help them. He thinks of piling up treasure only in the present life. But the day will come when he passes from time to eternity and, waking from his sleep, finds himself empty-handed.

Imitate, rather, the rich who are compassionate and humane; who become fathers to the poor; who are not afraid to impoverish themselves by giving alms freely.

How many blessings such men receive even on earth! Yet far more precious are the blessings they will receive in heaven.

Frequently the Lord gives back to them in overflowing measure? even on earth, what love has made them give away to the poor.

In addition, they may expect to have in eternity all the fullness He has promised.

If paradise had been closed to them because of their sins, almsgiving could open it to them. By almsgiving they could, as it were, make payment for their sins.

Make it your duty, then, to help the unfortunate. Do not give ear to your own cupidity which claims it never has enough. You are not forbidden to save, but you may not be hard-hearted and miserly. How praiseworthy it is to be thrifty so that one may help the poor!

Unless you are very poor, do not think you need give no alms. You must give alms according to your means. If you have a great deal, give a great deal; if you have but little, then gladly share that little with the poor.

My child, all who have practiced the works of mercy during their earthly lives will feel great confidence as they stand before the judgment seat of the God of mercy.

CHAPTER 4

NECESSITY AND ADVANTAGES OF MEDITATION

The Believer

O CAVE of Bethlehem, let me experience what Mary felt when the shepherds came to adore Jesus in the manger! Or rather, do you yourself, Virgin Mother, show me the thoughts and feelings that were in your heart at that moment.

Mary

My child, the deeply moving sight of God become an infant, bedded in a manger, and wrapped in poor rags was for me a wide and inexhaustibly deep theme for reflection. I could never weary of meditating on that great mystery. What I saw and heard was forever written in my heart and affected me profoundly. Even more than the shepherds did I wonder at the great things that were taking place; all the powers of my soul were concentrated on them. Countless tender affections sprang continuously from my heart, and I never ceased my praise and blessing of Almighty God.

My child, if you want a deeper understanding of the mysteries of faith you must take them seriously and meditate attentively on them.

Many Christians have but a weak faith because they neglect to nourish and strengthen it through meditation. The world is filled with so much crime and disorder, and the forgetfulness of the eternal truths is the reason for it. By meditating often on the perfections of God and the nothingness of things human the saints achieved detachment from creatures and were able to concentrate their affections on the Creator. Through this holy exercise they learned to value only what is great and valuable in God's eyes and their hearts were set on fire with a holy love that sought to lose itself in the bosom of God.

Therefore, let no day pass without feeding your soul on some salutary truth. That is how to learn the science of the saints. Do not excuse yourself with the claim that you have no time for meditation. What you lack is the will, not the time.

You have only one important business in life: to save your soul. Should you not think about it every day?

You always find time to think seriously about the transitory business of this world. And yet there are no concerns closer to you or of greater importance to you than those of eternity.

Do not excuse yourself by saying you cannot meditate. You are quite able to reflect on countless matters of pure curiosity. Can you really claim that you are unable to think when it comes to reflecting on the great mysteries of faith and eternity?

Admit rather that you have no great love for the Lord; admit that you are ungrateful.

My child, your life will always be well ordered if you examine yourself daily in the presence of God and if you are what you ought to be in His sight.

Death will surely not take you by surprise if you learn each day how to die well. Spend just a quarter of an hour each day meditating before the altar or your crucifix on the greatness, mercy, threats, and promises of the Lord, and you will acquire a knowledge infinitely superior to that of all the philosophers whose works teach everything but the knowledge of eternal salvation.

Of what use is it for a man to have stocked his mind with all the knowledge the world regards as practical and worthwhile if he lacks the knowledge the saints had, the knowledge that made them saints? You do not become virtuous simply by desiring it; you must seriously study and learn the means of becoming virtuous.

Never weary of asking Jesus for the grace to overcome your repugnance to an exercise from which the devil would gladly dissuade you, knowing as he does how important it is for you.

Do not deprive yourself of something so advantageous not only for yourself but for those who will be more especially entrusted to your care.

CHAPTER 5

OBSERVANCE OF GOD'S LAW

MARY had conceived through the action of the Holy Spirit and had become a mother without ceasing to be a virgin. Indeed, the birth of her Son served only to render her more pure. Consequently the law about purification did not apply to her. Yet she determined to observe it, and she did so with great care, omitting no detail.

The example of Jesus who had willed to submit Himself to the law of circumcision kept Mary from taking advantage of her privilege. Since there had been no exception made for the law of purification, Mary obeyed promptly and without human respect.

It might seem that in thus presenting her Son in the temple in accordance with the law she would risk having Him confused with the other children of men.

Yet the law bade mothers offer their firstborn sons to God in the temple. Mary did not think as she obeyed it that the heavenly Father would take care to manifest the glory of Jesus when He thought it opportune. Hers is an example that shames our cowardice in obeying God's law and shows up the emptiness of the excuses we use for dispensing ourselves from prompt and exact obedience.

It is a strange thing that we would dare deny God, the supreme Lord, the submission He requires of His subjects.

Dust and ashes though you are, you dare say to the greatest of masters, God Himself, that you are unable to obey and that His law asks too much of you since you are weak! How bold and rash you are!

How can you find the Lord's yoke too heavy when He Himself tells us that it is *easy and light* (Mt 11:30)? How can you prefer the world's yoke when it is far more tyrannical?

In obedience to the world men sacrifice all that is most precious to them: the years of their youth, their sharp minds, their hearts' affection, their powers and talents. Yet for obedience to the Lord they will set aside only some future time. That is, they will give Him only their declining years and the tattered remnants of their affections; in short, they will allow Him only what the world will someday no longer want.

To please the world we daily submit blindly to its whims and outlandish customs. Yet when it comes to pleasing the Lord and blindly obeying the laws of this kind master we find submission too difficult or we look for reasons to shake off His yoke.

If you look to your own or the world's interests before resolving to give God the obedience you owe Him, you will never obey, for God's law is contrary to your natural inclinations and to the world's ways.

It is not flesh and blood that you must consult when it comes to obeying God's law. Nature will only bid us claim weakness and the world will urge us to rebel.

Supreme Master, You alone have the right to command and no one has the right to ask You why. Open my heart to Your law! *Your words are just and equitable* (Ps 119:160). May they fall upon my heart *like the dew* (Deut 32:2).

Your Prophet tells us in one of his songs that abundant peace is stored up for those who love and obey Your law. He tells us that this law makes even the simplest wise, leads to genuine happiness, banishes sadness from the heart, enlightens the mind, is more desirable than gold or diamonds, and is sweeter than the sweetest honey (Ps 19).

I resolve once more never to depart from that law. Lord, please strengthen me in this resolve. I shall obey Your law until my last breath and shall think of it as a rich inheritance which I must carefully preserve and which will be my everlasting joy.

CHAPTER 6

GOOD EXAMPLE

MARY also observed the law of purification so that she might not scandalize her fellow Jews who did not know of her virginity. She observed it, moreover, in order to give Joseph and those to whom, like Joseph, God had revealed the mystery, an example of blind and generous obedience.

If a precept does not bind you, yet your failure to obey might scandalize others, then obey it, even if obedience requires a sacrifice of you. Even if obeying means leaving aside the sweetness of contemplation, do not hesitate. You are leaving the Lord for the Lord's sake.

Anyone who loves the Lord tries to win hearts to Him. But there is no better way to this than to show others by your good example how much you love Him yourself.

Exhortations to virtue can make people value it. But when example is joined to word, it persuades them to practice that virtue. The example of the saints makes saints.

The virtuous actions of the Apostles and first Christians were no less effective in converting men than their sermons and miracles.

How few Christians today become through virtuous example *the good fragrance of Jesus Christ* (2 Cor 2:15)!

We might almost think that men band together in society in order to contribute to each other's damnation through bad example!

If you want to damn yourself, then do it alone; do not drag with you the weak brothers for whom Jesus Christ has died!

If it is a crime to rob your neighbor of earthly possessions, how much greater a crime to rob him of eternal goods? Then you turn yourself into a messenger and tool of the devil.

All those especially who possess any authority tend to conform to the latter in the way they act.

This obligation lies especially heavy on the great. If such men do not respect the laws of God or the Church, they will be immediately imitated by others. Subjects may even regard it as something to boast about that they follow such example.

Let great men learn from the Virgin Mother of God to use their high position in order to give great glory to God who put them there.

Is earthly greatness to be justification for being less Christian? Of course not! Higher position, if you look at it correctly, only means a greater obligation.

CHAPTER 7

LOVE AND ESTEEM OF HUMILIATIONS

MY GOD, observance of the law of purification must have meant a deep humiliation for Your holy Mother, for that law was meant only for ordinary mothers.

The bright virginity for which she showed herself so solicitous at the Annunciation was in a sense obscured in this religious ceremony.

But she knew that shame and humiliation would one day be Your own lot, and she was happy to be able to resemble You.

The more You set her apart from other women, the more she wanted to be lost among them and to hide her special privileges.

A soul that like Mary seeks only to please God takes little account of esteem from men and is not greatly responsive to their homage. One of Your Prophets says it is better to be a lowly servant in the Lord's house than to have all the pomp and splendor with which the children of this world surround themselves.

Virtue is, in fact, safer in a lowly humble condition than amid honors and distinctions. If it is unknown and hidden from the eyes of man, it is all the more resplendent in God's sight.

True virtue alone has a claim on God's attention. If it is unknown to men or even scorned by them, it regards itself as all the more fortunate.

Providence that watches over the just often leads them by the path of humiliation to the goal of glorious reward.

Self-love undoubtedly suffers when we are humiliated, but the humiliation is only the more salutary for that reason.

The saints thanked God for the insults they suffered as for a special grace. If I do not feel the same way, it is because I am still a wholly earthly and fleshly man and therefore do not seek God.

Many saints have asked God for great humiliations because their desire of perfection was great. If I do not have the same courage, let me at least accept submissively the humiliations He sends me for my good.

I can honor the Lord more through a humiliation accepted with resignation to His will than through even the sublimest gift.

The Son of God humbled Himself, the Apostle tells us, even to the point of *emptying Himself* (Phil 2:7). That is the model I must try to imitate.

To have a horror of humiliation is to have a horror for the resemblance to Jesus which humiliation can give.

If God allows me many humiliations, it is because He wants to make the image of His Son perfect in me.

I ought to accept a humiliation with the same pleasure and gratitude I would have if I received a piece of the very cross of Jesus.

CHAPTER 8

HOW TO OFFER THE SACRIFICES GOD ASKS OF US

THE offering which mothers made of their first-born sons to God in the temple was but a small thing. However, your offering of Jesus, holy Virgin, was a true sacrifice.

You knew that someday He would sacrifice His life for the salvation of man. Therefore you offered Him now as a victim, just as He had already offered Himself to the eternal Father. The event in the temple was the beginning of sufferings that would last to the dying breath of Jesus.

Your soul would begin at that moment *to be pierced with the sword of sorrow* (Lk 2:35), of which Simeon spoke to you as he held Jesus in his arms.

The mothers of this world love their children, but the latter are not given all of their mothers' affection. How much affection these women reserve for empty things! How much for themselves! But you loved Jesus with all your power of loving; you loved Him with your whole heart and you loved Him alone. He was your only Son. You had hardly begun to taste the joy of being a mother, and the mother of such a son, when the day came for you to go and offer Him to His Divine Father, and you went.

Worthy daughter of Abraham and heir to his faith, you suppressed all your natural feelings and listened only to the voice of God Who wanted you to sacrifice what was dearest to you in this world.

Mary

My child, be persevering and generous like me when God asks anything of you, no matter what it may be.

He asked me to sacrifice what I loved the most.

Yet what does He ordinarily ask of you? Only the sacrifice of what you ought to hate!

If you love God, generosity should be the main proof of your love. A heart that is mean and niggardly does not know what it means to love. If you are unwilling to do anything difficult for God, if you lose heart at the sight of difficulties to be surmounted, can you be said to love? True love proves itself in pain and conflict. Inability to suffer is incompatible with the outlook and practice of an authentic follower of Jesus.

Do you want to please the Lord with your sacrifices? Then offer them promptly and without inquiring what they will cost you.

The world asks harder sacrifices of its disciples, yet it need only speak and they obey immediately and completely. Is God to be the only Lord to Whom no one is willing to offer sacrifice without first inquiring whether He is asking too much?

My child, we have but little love for God if we put limits to the proofs our love is willing to give.

In the world, a person who acts solely according to whim and loves only when it suits his interests would nonetheless not dare show a heart such as most Christians dare offer God.

A son who does only what his father absolutely requires, a wife who is not interested in pleasing her husband when pleasing him makes demands on her—do such people show a sincere and acceptable love?

God is infinitely good to all His creatures, but He is also *a jealous God* (Nah 1:2).

He is not served as He requires and deserves to be served unless He is served with a heart perfectly submissive to His every wish.

Be ashamed, then, to be so slow in His service! Be ashamed to do so little for Him when He has done so much for you.

Do you find that He gives you orders sometimes difficult to carry out? My child, He will give you other such orders, for you must earn His rewards!

Prosperity, rest, reputation, health, life itself: all these He may ask of you, for He has a right to them all.

Do not be surprised that the more you give Him, the more He will ask of you. He does this in order to prepare you for greater favors during your time on earth and to enable you to receive greater rewards in heaven.

CHAPTER 9

DISPOSITIONS OF SOUL IN TIME OF TRIAL

Mary

MY CHILD, why do you weep and sigh?

The Believer

Queen of the saints, I was just beginning to enjoy some little tranquility when suddenly I found myself troubled anew. Injustice, calumny, and ingratitude were plotting against me once more. Loving Mother, give this child of yours your help and protection.

Mary

My child, your state is somewhat like mine when I heard Simeon's prophecy there in the temple. After telling me of Jesus' future greatness, he predicted that He would meet opposition and persecution and that a sword of sorrow would pierce my heart (cf. Lk 2:34-33). Thus I would share the difficulties my Son would have to bear. I was very familiar, from Scripture, with the sufferings that would be Jesus' lot. Abel murdered, Joseph sold into slavery, David persecuted, and the paschal lamb were all figures foretelling what would befall Him.

What bitter grief I felt at the sufferings and death of Jesus, which were always in my thoughts! How I groaned within when I held Jesus to my breast and thought of the cruel death by which He must save the world! If I saw a lamb being slaughtered in the temple or a dove being sacrificed, I said to myself: "That is how Jesus will someday be offered."

The Believer

Virgin Mother, I glimpse how painful your state of mind must have been and why the Church rightly calls you "Queen of martyrs."

The martyrs were decapitated, exposed to wild animals, or perished by water or fire, but their torments were usually short, whereas yours lasted thirty-three years.

And during that whole time, filled with a courage and strength greater than those of all the martyrs, you heroically contemplated the ever new sufferings God was preparing for you and especially those you must someday endure on Calvary.

As for me, I am weakness itself and entirely cowardly before the evils that threaten me.

If your suffering was constantly renewed as you thought of the torments Jesus must undergo, you also continually renewed that first sacrificial offering you had made in the temple.

Your soul was weighed down by deep sadness, yet your peace was undisturbed. In perfect submission you wanted whatever God wanted. I, on the contrary, am frightened at the very thought of the new crosses He has in store for me. No more peace and tranquility for me! My spirit rebels and my heart complains.

Mary

My child, God will not allow you to be tempted, tested, or tormented beyond your strength. His help will always be equal to the trial He sends.

Give heed to His grace, for it already speaks to you, and respond to His inspirations. If God has more crosses in store for someone, He gives greater graces that the person may bear them.

Crosses are the most precious gifts God can give His creature; and the creature's acceptance of them is the most pleasing sacrifice it can offer its Creator.

If the crosses He intends for you are heavy, that means He has great plans for your sanctification. Do you want to prevent those divine plans being fulfilled?

Your disturbance and fears will not take the crosses from you, whatever you do; you must carry them. What, then, is the wiser thing for you to do?

It is to submit, my child, to all that God bids you do. You must say: The Lord is master; *let Him do with me as He thinks best* (cf. Lk 1:38).

Then you will see God moved by your submission; faithful to His promises, He will make lighter than you thought possible the crosses which from a distance seemed so heavy. He will make them so light that you will say: *Just as we share abundantly in the sufferings of Christ, so too, through Christ, do we receive consolation in equal measure* (2 Cor 1:5).

The Believer

Thank you, holy Mother, for the instruction you give me. It will strengthen me in my weakness.

It is you who obtain for me the new energy I feel within me for facing courageously the crosses I could not think of without trembling.

Praised be the Lord, my God, who through the instructions of His holy Mother readies my hand for the struggle and teaches me to endure a battle in which without such help I could not but be defeated.

CHAPTER 10

HOW TO ACT IN FACE OF GOD'S INSCRUTABLE PLANS

GOD unexpectedly told Mary, through Joseph to whom an angel had revealed it, that they must rescue the child Jesus from Herod's anger and set out for Egypt.

But God is infinitely powerful. Had He no way of changing the king's heart? Was it not unworthy of God to flee from a weak mortal?

Could He not have performed once again, this time for Jesus' sake, the miracle of the plagues with which He afflicted Egypt in order to save His people?

Mary was not concerned to try to understand God's plans in dealing with her.

So too His will deserves our submission, whether or not we understand why He acts as He does.

Mary did not ask whether she would have enough to eat during the long journey through the wilderness and the foreign land to which she was being sent.

The God Who gave the order to make the journey was powerful enough to enable her to find sustenance, though she might not see it readily.

Mary was not concerned to find out whether she would would have to stay in Egypt for a long period. She simply thought that she would return when God signalled the time for return.

God could give Mary orders even more difficult to understand than this one; she would never lose her tranquility.

And indeed, what is there that should trouble a soul that knows God is its guide? Is there perhaps some surer protection than that which Divine Providence offers?

Prayer

Lord, you bid me travel by paths I do not know. Your command is enough for me; Your will is my light and all the reason I need. Admittedly I do not know where I am going, but I am sure that if I let myself be led by a guide as wise as You are I shall not go astray.

Although I walk in darkness, I walk with assurance, for I am sure You will not desert me.

Of what use would my own weak light be on a path where You Yourself are my guide and which You order me to follow in blind obedience? You have spoken; I must act without listening to myself.

We often trust entirely the advice of a man who is regarded as prudent and enlightened. Have we any reason for mistrust when You, eternal wisdom, are the one who directs us?

Therefore, however surprising I may find Your plans for me, I shall simply bow down before them in adoration, for Your power surpasses my power to understand it.

Your action, even when hidden, is no less to be adored. Your works all bear the stamp of infinite wisdom, even when their secret is not revealed.

I wish, then, to be no less submissive to Your commands, even when I do not understand the reason for them, than I am to the truth You have revealed to me. I do not comprehend that truth, yet I am surer of it than if I understood it by my own powers, for it is You, Lord, Who have spoken.

CHAPTER 11

GOD'S CARE FOR THE DEVOUT

The Believer

OBEDIENT Virgin, I recall with joy the tranquil confidence in God that was yours as you learned that you must set out for Egypt.

You were sure that God, Who guided you always, would watch over you throughout the journey and would not abandon you when you reached the place He had chosen for your journey's end.

Could He fail to watch over you and the holy one He had entrusted to your care?

Of course not! *You will not fear the terror by night nor the arrow that flies by day. . . . For He will command His angels about you—to guard you wherever you go. They will lift you up with their hands, lest you injure your foot against a stone. You will tread upon the asp and the viper; you will trample the lion and the dragon* (Ps 91:5, 11-13).

Mary

My child, in many passages of Sacred Scripture the Lord promises to protect those who trust in Him.

Never let yourself be dismayed, then, as you carry out His commands, however difficult they may be. Hope in Him and He will help you.

Even when obedience to His will brings with it the danger of dire need, *cast all your anxiety on Him, because He cares deeply about you* (1 Pet 5:7).

Should you be exposed to the sneers and insults and persecution of malicious men, do not lose heart, *for the Lord is a refuge for the oppressed, a refuge in times of distress* (Ps 9:10).

The trust which upright men place in Him is an infallible guarantee that He will protect them.

If at times He seems to abandon them for a brief space, you will see that at the last moment He restores their peace and tranquility.

The citizens of Bethulia no longer expected anything of the God of their fathers, but His providential care was more attentive than ever to their needs.

Chaste Joseph was not forgotten by Divine Providence. Condemned to prison and oblivion, he groaned in his chains, but he was unexpectedly released and elevated to the highest honors, even receiving a share in supreme authority.

But Providence does not always liberate the upright from all fear and danger, nor does it always give them in their need the kind of help they want and ask for. But its plans are no less wonderful, whether it releases men from need or leaves them in it, whether it avenges them against injustice or leaves them to be its victims.

In affliction God gives them the grace to be patient, and thereby bestows a greater blessing on them than if He were to overwhelm them with prosperity.

Even today, how many Christians there are who lack everything, yet seem to need nothing, so great is their contentment!

Such men bless God for His providence and would not change places with those whom the world regards as supremely fortunate.

Have recourse to the Lord, therefore, in your every need; abandon yourself entirely to Him. The help you receive may not always be clear and startling, but it will nonetheless be real and strengthening.

CHAPTER 12

IN ALL CIRCUMSTANCES THE LORD CAN BE SERVED

Mary

MY CHILD, why do you complain about your state and situation? You say that in them you cannot serve the Lord as you ought? But heaven is filled with saints who became saints in circumstances like yours.

I found God in Egypt, to which I had to move, just as I had found Him in Judea, and I managed to serve Him as before.

If we can preserve the grace and friendship of God in a situation, then we ought to be content with it.

I found it very hard to leave Israel, as did my husband Joseph, but we felt no regret.

Again, when we were summoned back to our home, the only pleasure we felt was at doing the Lord's will, for that was at all times our only law.

My child, if you seek to do the heavenly Father's will and not your own and are content with the state in which He has placed you, you will desire nothing else.

God has blessed the way each person must travel toward sanctity, and you would err if you thought you could find holiness by choosing some other way.

No one can be holy without the help of grace. Now, God grants His grace to each person according as it is needed for the kind of life to which He calls him and the duties for which He destines him.

One who has withdrawn into solitude should not be saddened at having left the world behind, and one whose duty places him in the world should not say he cannot be saved there. The safest state for each is the one in which God has placed him.

Whatever be the situation in which we find ourselves, our salvation depends on fidelity to grace.

John the Baptist found holiness on the banks of the Jordan, where God wanted him to stay. He did not seek to go elsewhere.

The kind of life led by the Apostles who accompanied Jesus and received His teaching did not seem to them any less suitable than John's for reaching holiness.

No, your state is not of itself a barrier to holiness. For it is not the place nor the occupation that sanctifies a man; it is the man who must sanctify the place and the occupation.

We often turn our thoughts to some state other than the one in which we are. The reason, however, is not love of goodness but our restlessness.

What gain would you have in changing? Would you be a better person? No: in changing your situation or condition, you might change your mood, but not your character.

Wherever we go, our defects follow us. My child, what you must change is not your state or your duties but yourself.

Sanctify what you do in your present state by referring it all to God, and you will not have cause to complain that your duties are a source of distraction.

The many tasks required by the administration of a great kingdom did not prevent David from praying and from singing the Lord's praises seven times each day.

Numerous occupations did not prevent the saints from becoming saints; instead, they sanctified their occupations.

Holiness does not consist in serving God where and as you would like, but where and as He wishes.

You will glorify God more on a bed of pain if it be His will that you lie there, than if you were to wear yourself out with hard work in an effort to win souls to Him.

CHAPTER 13

FERVOR IN GOD'S SERVICE

The Believer

HOLY Virgin, in every situation of your life that has been made known to us you gave us splendid examples of fervent piety.

It was that fervent devotion that yearly brought you to Jerusalem at Passover time.

Although the obligation of going up to celebrate this great festival lay only on your husband Joseph, you never failed to accompany him.

Your love of God was too great to permit your doing for Him only what was strictly duty.

How ungrateful I am! And how differently I have acted toward the Lord up to now! De spite all His benefits to me I have always shown myself niggardly to Him, and if He wanted my

obedience and homage He had to command
me as my Lord.

Mary

My child, a heart that loves God neglects
nothing it can do to please Him.

You have little realization of how much the
Lord deserves your service, if you are unwilling
to put yourself out for Him.

Consider how much those who declare
themselves followers of the world are willing to
do for their master, and learn from them what
you should be willing to do for the Lord.

See how concerned they are: they spare
themselves neither suffering nor weariness in
serving the world and, only to please it, condemn themselves to a thousand forms of sub-
jection.

Yet you find it too heavy a burden to please
God and give this sovereign master proofs of
your love. To ask you to be attentive to His will
is to ask of you a submission that is too great.

Do you not find it humiliating that I am
forced to call your attention to the example of
worldlings and to send you to school with
them in order to learn how to serve God?

Let not the children of this world outstrip
you in generosity and let the world not boast
that it is better served by its followers than the

God of Christians is by those who claim to belong to Him!

Stop being one of those Christians who think themselves very devout if they do exactly what the law prescribes under threat of punishment.

These people give the impression that they would easily consent to losing God's grace if they could do it without risk of punishment. They fear God rather than love Him.

My child, you should indeed fear this God Whose punishments are terrible, but you should fear, more than anything else, that you may not love enough this God Who is so good and lovable.

Would a friend think you a very fervent friend of his if you were willing to do only what friendship absolutely required?

Love is generous and will not be limited to what it is obliged to do. If you love greatly, you use every opportunity to please the one you love.

If your love for God is fervent, then whatever you do for Him will be less than what you want to do.

Love ardently and your love will alleviate your weariness. To a fervent soul God gives such a desire that it finds heavenly delight even in what costs it the most effort.

The Believer

Dear loving Mother, win for me from your Son the fervor of which you speak and of which you have given me such glowing examples!

I admit it with shame: every difficulty stops me; I yield to the first temptation of boredom and disgust; and human respect often prevents me from carrying out the inspirations of grace.

You see how much I need encouragement. May your salutary instructions kindle in my heart the fervent love the God of love deserves to find in His servant!

CHAPTER 14

THE MISFORTUNE OF LOSING JESUS

WHEN Jesus was twelve years old Mary and Joseph took Him to Jerusalem for the Passover.

When the celebration was over Mary and Joseph returned to Nazareth while Jesus remained by Himself in Jerusalem. On the way home, after a day's journey Mary and Joseph discovered that Jesus was no longer with them.

What anxiety His absence must have caused them! What sorrow Mary especially must have felt at losing Jesus!

But, my Savior, Mary had not lost You through her fault. You had left her in order to devote Yourself to Your Father's business. I, on the contrary, have often lost You through my own fault because of my sins. I often forced You to abandon me, and I should have felt great sorrow at this loss and abandonment.

Mary, give me a share of your sorrow. I need it, and you do not!

Mary had lost only the bodily presence of Jesus; His friendship for her was untouched. But I lost the dearest thing in all the world: the grace and friendship of Jesus.

Could the world and its pleasures, which I had preferred to Jesus, make up to me for my immense loss?

Happy they from whom Jesus has never had to withdraw and who have always possessed Him! They alone know and can tell us what paradise on earth is.

How sweet the company of Jesus is! How pleasant to converse with Him and tell each other of our affection! What a Divine joy!

But what a fearful solitude when one is separated from Him! What dark night and terrible need! What a hell on earth!

If the man who has lost Jesus really knew his own misfortune, he would gladly give all the world's riches and honors and pleasures to find Him again.

Men shed tears and are even inconsolable at temporal losses. Yet they weep not but are insensible to the loss of God Himself! Can a Christian suffer any greater loss than this?

Men never suffer temporal loss without regret. It is only You, my God, the infinite good, that they lose without shedding a single tear of sorrow! How little they love You!

Can a wife live on in tranquility when she has lost the most loving of husbands?

Can a child feel no pain when he has lost the best of parents?

Father of mercies (2 Cor 1:3), restore Your friendship to Your child! Divine Spouse of our souls, give us back Your love!

Be moved, Lord, by the tears that pour from my eyes!

I feel horror at myself when I think that I have deserved to lose You Who have given me such striking proofs of Your love for me and of the pleasure You find in seeing me near You.

What a narrow heart I have when it comes to detesting my ingratitude! Yet all the hearts of men together could not conceive such a hatred of my sins as to equal my misfortune in committing them.

But if I am the worst of ingrates, Your mercy, for which I beg, is even greater. It will supply for the repentance I lack and would like to have.

I wish my repentance were as great as the faith that enlightens me and teaches me the infinite abhorrence I ought to have for sin and the infinite love I ought to have for You.

I see how unworthy my actions have been, and I would feel it less if You were less good.

My ingratitude has no power to weary Your patience. You have waited for me with a pity I can never marvel at enough and can never be grateful enough for.

In the deplorable condition I find myself before You, what motive for hope can I have except Your goodness? Jesus, my Savior, when You restore me to Your friendship, You show me how great Your mercy is.

I know I have merited severe punishment at Your just hands. Punish this rebel! But give him back the place he had in Your heart! Take from me all that can bind me to the world: possessions and fortune, honor and reputation, the esteem and friendship of men. But let me not again suffer the misfortune of losing You.

In the future may I make up, through a faithful and ardent love, for the lost time when I lived far off from You.

Jesus, bring me near You, for Your heart is always the same, always open to receive us despite our sins.

In Your heart I long to take refuge. Let me not go forth from it again but dwell in it for all eternity!

CHAPTER 15

HOW AND WHERE TO SEEK JESUS WHEN LOST

AS SOON as Mary realized that Jesus was no longer with them, she hastened to look for Him, first among those nearby, then in Jerusalem, and had the good fortune to find Him there.

The joy she felt at finding her beloved Son again was no less than the anxiety His absence had caused her.

My soul, you too have lost Jesus! Therefore imitate the concern of this loving Mother and, like her, leave all else in order to find Him.

Lamenting and tearful, you should inquire concerning Him of every creature, of heaven and earth, of the light of day and the darkness of the night.

Men often seek Jesus and do not find Him because they do not seek Him as He should be sought. Some even seek Him as though they would be displeased to find Him!

Your readiness to look for Him and your haste to find Him should be proof of the sorrow you feel at having lost Him.

But where will you find Him? Amid the world? No, for Jesus has declared Himself its enemy.

Do not delude yourself that flesh and blood will help you find Him. Mary and Joseph *looked for Him among their relatives and friends but failed to find Him* (Lk 2:44-45).

Consult rather the teachings of the gospel, inquire of the saints, ask the ministers of the Lord, and they will tell you where to find Him.

You will find Jesus where Mary found Him: *in the temple* (Lk 2:46), in the house of prayer, in the company of His ministers and servants. You will also find Him in solitude, through practices of devotion, especially in the solitude of the heart, which means in the silence of the passions and in recollection.

He Himself invites you to betake yourself there and listen to His voice that you may hear *the words of eternal life* (Jn 6:68), which issue from His lips. There is where He has been sought, and is still sought, by those who sincerely wish to draw near to Him, whether they have wandered far from Him through a perverse and sinful life or have simply lost sight of Him through lukewarmness and deliberate dissipation.

My soul, when you find Him, what peace will be yours! Did you ever find any happiness when you were far from Him?

The man who has found Jesus suddenly discovers from his own experience that so great a treasure was worth all the trouble it took to find.

CHAPTER 16

HOW TO ACT AFTER FINDING JESUS

The Believer

MARY, immediately after finding Jesus you took Him back to Nazareth. What a happiness for you! Even the angels envied you.

With what motherly care you watched over this priceless treasure! With what greater concern than ever you guarded His life and person!

Mary

My child, it is indeed a great honor to find Jesus once again, and we should omit no care to retain possession of Him.

The Believer

Holy Virgin, teach me what I ought to do, that I may not find myself again deprived of this supreme good.

Mary

My child, look closely at the reason why Jesus departed from you and how you managed to lose His grace and turn Him into an enemy.

Did you not begin to grow lukewarm in His service and to commit many faults that made Him unhappy with you? Through repeated neglect you gradually built up a wall of separation between Jesus and yourself.

Did you not grow fond of some dangerous passion and fail to extinguish it as soon as you saw its first spark appear in your heart?

When God asked you to sacrifice some overly human attachment and affection, did you not refuse?

When we refuse the sacrifices the Lord asks of us, we remove ourselves from a quite special providence that safeguards us against wandering far from Him.

If you recognize that one of these faults or some other took you away from Jesus, look for the source of the evil. If you are to remove the effect, you must remove the cause.

Watch over yourself more carefully. Watch over your heart with all possible care and never go outside it. The heart cannot be influenced without danger to you; the very life of the soul depends on guarding your heart.

Be faithful in little things lest you become unfaithful in great things. Neglect of little faults leads gradually to serious defects.

Jesus does not want a heart that is divided. He has made your heart entirely for Himself and wants to possess it in its entirety.

My child, the little faults for which you, like so many paltry souls, pardon yourself so easily gradually take you away from Jesus and Him from you.

They do not cause a break with Him, but they prepare for such a break; the Lord looks on them as so many proofs of your coldness, and such coldness lessens the number of His graces.

Fidelity maintains the exchange of affection between the heart of Jesus and the heart of the upright man. Live with Jesus as you want Him to live with you. You want Him to pour out on you the riches of His love; then open your heart to Him without reserve.

Reserve toward Him shows a mean heart. The love you have for anything else makes Him jealous. The least word spoken to Him by one who loves Him is well received. With the same dispositions of faithful love you should in turn receive the inspirations of Jesus, whether He is suggesting through His grace some means of avoiding sin, or suggesting means of deepening your virtue.

The Believer

Holy Virgin, you know perfectly what love and fidelity are! Help me, with the grace of God, to derive profit from your instruction.

But, weak as I am, shall I not have the misfortune of losing Jesus again and forever?

Mary

My child, it is right that you should fear; if you did not, I would try to inspire you with fear.

But this fear should not be accompanied by disturbance and disquiet of soul, but should instead be moderated by confidence.

On your part, do everything that depends on you to persevere in love of Jesus, and expect from His goodness the grace of perseverance.

The Believer

My dear Mother, what a terrible uncertainty for the soul that fears nothing so much as not persevering, when God leaves it ignorant of whether or not it will persevere!

Mary

My child, that is the lot of all who are still in this life.

God has determined that it should be so, lest you be shipwrecked on the reef of presumption.

The uncertainty should keep you humble, inspire you with a holy distrust of yourself, and make you work out your salvation in fear and trembling.

Only in heaven can we be free of all fear and enjoy the happy certainty of being always with Jesus.

CHAPTER 17

THE FAITHFUL MAN SHOULD NOT BE DISCOURAGED IN DESOLATION AND DRYNESS

AT TIMES God treats the upright man in a way that disturbs and alarms him. He wants to test his fidelity and therefore deprives him for a while of His sensible presence. This is how Jesus acted toward His holy Mother. He had foreseen the anxiety His absence would cause, yet He left her for a while and, unknown to her, remained in the Temple.

Christian soul, if it pleases this God of love to test you in the same way, be not dismayed. Arm yourself with courage and wait patiently for His return.

He is always near you to help you when you ask for His help, but it is good that He should pretend at times to depart from you, so that you may realize how unfortunate you would be if you really lost Him.

When He favors a person with consolations, it is in order to strengthen him in his trials. When He permits him to be left in dryness and desolation, it is in order that he may not grow proud of the goodness God shows him.

All or almost all His friends have experienced such alternations of joy and sorrow, consolation and dryness, peace and temptation.

When Jesus seemed to depart from them and abandon them to themselves, they felt all their weakness. But they did not lose heart, for they knew that His presence is not always sensibly felt and because they were sure He would help them.

They knew that God foresees the difficulties we must endure and that He has given us the means of drawing profit from them.

When His grace was sustaining you in sweetness and consolation, you advanced with pleasure and ease. Yet you make greater progress in virtue when you experience dryness and bear with patience, humility, and submission the state of abandonment in which God seems to have left you.

This state is indeed one of sadness, for we fear it is more of a punishment than a test. But, Christian soul, when you find yourself in it, do not lose confidence. Hope always, hope firmly, and the trial will not be long, any more than it was for Mary.

Imitate the solicitude of this Divine Mother as she searched for her Son. Seek Him, as she did, with a holy desire and a holy impatience to find Him.

Never complain, for Jesus owes you nothing, and if you must lament, let it be a lament of love, like Mary's.

"Son," she said, *"why have you done this to us? Your father and I have been searching for you with great anxiety"* (Lk 2:48).

Tell Him simply: "My Jesus, why have you put me to such a hard test. You know how I suffer from Your absence!

"Is it some infidelity of mine that has merited Your departing so far from me?

"If I have deserved it by actions that displeased You, pardon me, Lord. Henceforth I shall be more attentive to avoid anything that can displease You. But, whatever be Your reason for acting this way toward me, I accept the trial as You wish me to accept it and for as long as You wish, provided You let me always keep love of You in my heart."

CHAPTER 18

THE HIDDEN LIFE

The Believer

HOLY Virgin, explain to me the mystery of the hidden life you led at Nazareth. For, had you shown yourself to the world, you could have won great honors and many hearts for Jesus.

Mary

My child, my glory was to imitate Jesus who wished to be a *hidden God* (Isa 45:15) for a long period of His earthly life. He had come into the world in order to teach men to flee human glory and practice humility. By His hidden life at Nazareth He wanted to teach them by example before teaching them by word.

The heavenly Father wanted to be glorified by the hidden life of Jesus, and Jesus Himself preferred that obscurity to the miracles He could do. In this way He taught us that perfection and merit do not always consist in doing great things for the Lord, but in occupying ourselves, if it be His will, in daily toil and in humble duties which the world scorns.

He wanted to show us that we deceive ourselves if we believe it takes extraordinary deeds for a man to become holy.

By His hidden life He wanted, above all, to condemn the great concern many Christians have to show everyone their virtues and to win esteem, applause, and honor.

My child, love to be hidden, ignored, forgotten. As long as you have God's approval, what does the world's approval matter? The world passes away, and with it all the things of the world.

At Nazareth, I had Jesus, I had His love and He had mine. What more did we need to be happy?

A little corner of earth, where you might live entirely alone without any company but your crucifix, should seem more desirable to you than the palaces of kings.

There you would tap the source of repentant tears and cleanse yourself more completely of your sins. There you would be more intimately united to Jesus and have, in His love, a foretaste of heaven's joys.

The hidden life seems gloomy to you because you have never tasted its sweetness. If you once began to taste it you would find the world's honors and pleasures an empty thing, and emptier still those who seek them.

In such a life you must indeed often put up with mockery of worldly people who are amazed that you should scorn their amusements. But their sneers prove very useful, since they lead to a closer union with Jesus, the sole object of our desires.

My child, few men live in peace of conscience and spiritual joy, because few love to withdraw from the crowd and dwell alone with Jesus.

We often see men who seem virtuous but in fact have no solid piety. This is because they go out of themselves too much and like to show themselves in public.

They are spiritual only in their words; in their actions they are worldly. Grace does not dwell for long in a dissipated soul, a soul that seeks to attract any other gaze than that of the heavenly Spouse.

Ask Jesus for the vivid light He grants His saints so that they may realize the happiness of a life *hidden with Christ in God* (Col 3:3).

CHAPTER 19

THE INTERIOR LIFE

PARTICULARLY appropriate to Mary were these words uttered by the Holy Spirit: *All the beauty of the king's daughter is within* (Ps 45:14).

What we know of her outward actions is nothing as compared with what went on within her soul.

Imagine the Virgin Mother in her house at Nazareth and enter into her soul to study it.

Who could express her affections, her sentiments, her desires? Who could describe what went on in that holy sanctuary? You alone, my God, had taken possession of all the powers of her soul. You alone were the origin and end of her every action.

You were continually present to her mind, and she saw You in every creature. Nothing could distract her from You, for You were all in all to her.

Her judgments were guided by the principles of eternal wisdom; her actions were directed by Your Spirit; her words were inspired by love of You.

Free of every profane entanglement, Mary attended to God and her domestic duties with the freedom of a soul that is liberated from all purely human thoughts and worries.

Through a special grace Mary had a sure mastery of all the movements of her heart; yet she took the most scrupulous care to keep it free of any distraction.

She would have rejected any affection, intention, or desire that was not directed to God and to His glory.

From such a model we can see that the interior life consists in watching over oneself and one's heart, so that all affections and thoughts are consecrated to God.

This watchfulness is like an eye kept always open to distinguish between what comes from nature so that it may be suppressed, and what comes from grace so that we may conform ourselves to it.

Through such watchfulness as this we win the grace and strength never to subject ourselves to the impulses of nature. Without it we commit many faults and even lapses. With it, we will frequently perform great acts of virtue. without doing anything outwardly extraordinary.

How many holy hermits and virgins have reached the heights of sanctity simply through the merits of an interior life!

You will never taste the peace and joy the Holy Spirit gives if you are not an interior man.

The interior man is able to be master of himself; and as he watches over himself so as to free himself from the attacks which stir the passions and subject the soul, so also he preserves peace of heart even amid events that would overwhelm an ordinary degree of patience.

The man given to externals, on the contrary, is anxious and agitated by countless trifles that are unworthy of his attention, and so he loses peace and tranquility. The interior man acknowledges only the wisdom that shows him the nothingness of earthly things and thus raises his eyes and his thoughts to the contemplation of heavenly things.

The man given to externals consults only the prudence of the flesh. All that seems to violate that prudence is darkness or even madness, in his eyes. The one man is constantly on guard against the illusions and seductions of the senses; the other always judges and acts according to the senses and refers everything to them.

Find your delight in thinking of God, seeking Him in everything, doing all for Him; then you will have *the kingdom of God within you* (Lk 17:21).

You will be that *true worshiper* of whom Jesus speaks, who *"worships the Father in Spirit and truth"* (Jn 4:23).

Why is the majority of mankind always agitated and always complaining? Because it lives a wholly external life and is occupied solely with the things of earth.

The people who by their way of life seem to be always with God are often not what they seem to be. Their heart is divided up between a crowd of useless affections; their mind is distracted by a multitude of empty thoughts.

God alone occupies the thoughts of the interior man; God alone occupies his intentions and his heart. Nothing else, however splendid, moves him.

We should regulate the exterior in accordance with the interior. But most men invert the order; for them the exterior regulates and perverts the interior.

Try, then, to remain within yourself and give yourself to external affairs only when God requires it. Even then, follow the attractions of grace which will summon you into yourself to examine your affections and intentions.

Do not believe that the interior life is proper only to certain states and times. It is compatible with the duties of any state of life and with even the most absorbing occupations.

It can be practiced in adversity as well as in prosperity, in sickness as well as in health, in action as well as in rest, in times of upset and trial as well as in times of calm and peace.

There is no situation in which we cannot enter into ourselves and examine what is going on there.

Above all, however, apply yourselves to the practices of the interior life if God calls you to apostolic work.

If you neglect this means of perfection, you will get too involved in external things and seek yourself rather than God. On the other hand, God will not want to use you to help souls make progress because you cannot teach others to practice what you yourself hardly practice.

CHAPTER 20

SILENCE

The Believer

I TURN to you, Queen of all the virtues, to learn when to be silent and when to speak. You practiced the virtue of silence in a perfect way. Let me learn from you how to practice it.

The Gospel records few of your words for us. You never spoke except to show men some virtue.

What love of purity, what humility and submission we see in the words you spoke to the angel when he came to greet you in the name of the adorable Trinity! In Elizabeth's house you spoke only to thank God for His favors. When you found Jesus in the Temple, you spoke to tell Him of your maternal love, and you spoke at the wedding feast of Cana in order to meet the needs of others which love had made your own.

But you kept silence on many occasions when it seemed you should have expressed your thoughts to people close to you.

For witness to the marvels that accompanied the birth of Jesus we must go the account given of them by His first worshipers.

Nothing that they said escaped you, but, as the Evangelist points out, you *treasured all these words and pondered them in your heart* (Lk 2:19).

In the Temple after presenting the Child Jesus you kept a wonderful silence that is a lesson for us. Later you went forth with Jesus to Calvary and stood at the foot of His Cross; you heard His final breath; during all that time you kept the perfect silence of patience and resignation to God's will.

Mary

My child, my silence itself speaks to you, and all devout souls understand its language well.

We should speak only when circumstances or the glory of God or love for our neighbor requires it. Apart from these cases it is better to be silent. In silence we find the spirit of recollection and the grace of God which is its source. We learn that to be recollected and interior people we must speak but little, and then say what the Spirit tells us in our heart we ought to say.

Readiness to speak too much is the sign of a distracted heart and mind, and such distraction is already a great evil.

Sentiments of piety easily vanish in the course of conversation; silence on the contrary preserves and strengthens them.

You will find few people who repent of having kept silence, but many who regret having said too much.

The wise man speaks only when *the right moment comes* (Sir 20:6), that is, when silence would be wrong or unfitting.

The man who cannot guard his tongue is *like a city whose walls are broken down* (Prov 25:28), exposed on all sides to the surprise attacks of the enemy.

Wherever many words are spoken, sin is not lacking (Prov 10:19). The man who speaks less is always the more prudent.

Constant experience tells us that where there is greater silence, there is greater innocence. Remember the principle that it is always better to remain silent when there is no need to speak. It is a great art to be able deliberately to speak or remain silent, and men can be quite expert in everything else but ignorant here. Grace gives us better instruction than all the teachings of men.

My child, the less you speak to creatures, the more God will speak to your heart. Think of the countless useless things that ordinarily are the subject of the world's conversation as being an obstacle to the holy relationship God wishes to

have with you. Above all, say little to men
about your afflictions and difficulties, for they
are not as interested in them as you may think.
Rather, speak much of them to God Who is
always ready to console you. If your crosses
have been caused by men, do not tell them to
anyone unnecessarily. You will often have
cause for regret if you say too much.

CHAPTER 21

UNION WITH GOD

The Believer

G OD of charity and love, may You be forever praised for the close relationship You
deigned to establish with the Virgin You had
chosen as Mother of our Savior.

And may you, holy Virgin, be praised as you
deserve for having faithfully corresponded to
God's grace. I cannot weary of admiring your
sublime virtues; but what especially excites my
wonder is your intimate and unbroken union
with Him.

Your heart, free as it was of all affections
toward creatures, was like a mystical heaven within which the Lord loved to dwell and where you
enjoyed His presence in peace. Sleep did not
interrupt this sweet relationship, and you could
say, with the bride of the Song of Songs, *"I sleep,
but my heart is awake"* (Song 5:2).

Why is it not given to me to live united to God in this way and to be bound to earth only by the bonds of the body?

Mary

My child, it was a great grace the Lord gave me that I should never lose awareness of His presence.

If you aspire to the same favor, begin by doing away with all earthly affections and separating yourself from all that is not God. The effort will be a costly one, but you can never pay too dearly for the gift that will reward your efforts and sacrifices.

Make use of everything around you to elevate your mind to God, and you will find countless reasons for glorifying and praising Him.

The heavens, that stretch so majestically above you, *proclaim the glory of God* (Ps 19:2); the sparkling of the stars is an image of His splendor; the vast extent of the oceans gives you an idea of His immensity; all the beings scattered throughout nature speak of His perfections; everything, even the smallest flower of the field, is like an open book set before your eyes to tell you of Him.

You can find God without going out of yourself, for you do not have life or movement or existence except in Him and from Him.

It is God Who enlightens your mind, moves your will, and makes your heart beat, and asks you for that heart in the tenderest and most affectionate way.

This God of all goodness watches over you to protect you and commands nature constantly to help you in your need.

There is no need, then, to look for Him far off from you. Enter into yourself, become aware of His holy presence, and He will cause you to experience it in many ways.

He will do it at times through unexpected enlightenment, and at other times through brilliant thoughts, hidden impulses, pious sentiments, and loving reproofs of your infidelity.

Avoid putting obstacles in the way of these varied effects of grace by any levity of mind and boredom of will.

Take up the practices that can best lead you to God, and fulfill your obligations in a religious spirit.

In your ordinary actions and the duties of your state, act in keeping with the intentions of providence.

Even in holy things do nothing hurriedly, for precipitation, too, can hinder the inner harmony which alone unites man to God.

When you find yourself filled with joy or sorrow, do not follow the impulse of nature or

MARY GIVES BIRTH TO JESUS

"[Mary] gave birth to her firstborn Son. She wrapped Him in swaddling clothes and laid Him in a manger" (Luke 2:7).

open your heart to creatures, but only to God. Love to share with Him what saddens or rejoices you, looking upon Him as a father and friend before whom you can confidently lay the causes of your suffering, your joys, and your contentment.

It is especially through this interior intimacy that you will win His heart and approach that holy union which is the sweetest enchantment life holds for the Christian soul.

CHAPTER 22

DUTIES OF STATE

GOD rarely asks us to prove our love for Him with striking deeds. That love is rather to be shown through constant fidelity to the smallest duties of our state.

Through such fidelity Mary acquired merits that would raise her above the angels.

She remained hidden for thirty years at Nazareth with the Savior. There her chief concern was to raise her Divine Son, to merit increasingly the confidence of her husband, and to provide her family with what they needed by working as her strength allowed.

Imitate her example if you want to reach holiness.

It is a mistake to associate holiness with practices different from the duties of our state and to neglect the latter in order to do the former. The greatest of all perfections is to love one's own state and to carry out its obligations, however ordinary they may be, when this state is in conformity to the order established by Divine Providence.

A worker who earns his bread by the sweat of his brow or the father of a family who, without worldly ambition, lives in the obscurity of modest means, is doing no less for his salvation (and often with less risk) than those who are in some higher state or even those who exercise the holiest of ministries.

The best state for you is not the one you think perfect but the one in which God has placed you.

It is an illusion to want to be holy in your own way and not in the way God determines. A thing is done perfectly only if it is done the way God wants it and because He wants it.

The merit of our actions depends relatively little on the nature of the things we do, and very much on the spirit in which we do it and on its conformity with God's will.

God wants of us a continuous series of little actions, while you want to do some great ones. The only result, if you follow your own way, is that you will do neither the small nor the great well.

Martha, Martha, you are anxious and upset about many things (Lk 10:41), and you deceive yourself in wanting to do more than God intends.

Be content to do as much good as He asks of you, and put into it the same fervor you would have if you were doing something great.

What great things did that courageous woman do whose praises the Holy Spirit sings? She wove and did the other little things that must be done in a household.

To go to church, pray, and visit the sick are fine things, but if you do them when the duties of your state require something far different of you, can you claim to be doing God's will?

We need to pray, and pray often; we need to pray always as far as that is possible; but if you neglect your domestic duties in order to pray, your prayer does not please God.

How many good works do not rise up to heaven because they are done simply to satisfy a man's self-will! On the other hand, what treasures of merit are produced by the actions of an ordinary everyday life because they are all signed with the seal of the Divine Will!

Many who do not think of themselves as acquiring great virtue will nonetheless be exalted higher in heaven than they expect. It will be because of the fidelity they showed in even the smallest duties of their state.

The master of whom the Gospel speaks says to his servant: *"Come and share your master's joy,"* not because you have done great things, but *"because you have been faithful in small matters"* (Mt 25:21).

CHAPTER 23

HOW TO SANCTIFY OUR DAILY TOIL AND ACTIONS

Mary

M Y CHILD, the duties of your state are much on your mind; yet in carrying them out you do not stop even for a moment to think of God.

The Believer

Virgin ever faithful and watchful, teach me how I, like you, can be united to God during my work and the fulfillment of the duties of my state.

Mary

Manual work and even occupations that are more burdensome and irksome cannot distract a spiritual and interior man from union with God.

A soul that is habitually recollected has a great facility in remembering God, even on occasions when the duties of his state would seem inevitably to cause some dissipation of attention.

The purity of intention with which he sanctifies every action, and continuous offering of it to God, enable him to avoid the kinds of dissipation into which less attentive souls slip.

The spirit of faith and religion ennobles, sweetens, and consecrates everything. Any thing done in such a spirit is an action that pleases God and is judged by Him to be worthy of His rewards.

Such a man does for God what so many others do simply for the world's sake or for some temporal advantage. Occupy yourself with what your state requires, but do it for Christian motives. Then you will have worked for both time and eternity.

But if you set to work out of pleasure or whim, compulsion or habit, or any other purely human motive, and God is not the reason why you act, you will pass whole hours without even once turning your affections to Him.

Do not say you cannot think of two things at the same time: a heart says to God in a moment what it really wants to say to Him.

I worked for Jesus and I was not distracted from my work when I spoke to Him.

In the midst of your occupations you speak of them to those who are near. Then speak of them to your God as well, for He is present to all you do. His conversation, unlike so many conversations of man, has nothing in it to displease or bore.

You can taste His sweetness in any occupation whatsoever.

You can become a great saint simply by doing ordinary things, but doing them in no ordinary way.

Most men apply themselves to what they do, only because they must. To do it because God commands, and do it with the intention of pleasing Him, is something they never think of.

As for you, my child, when you work, tell Him that you find your delight in doing His will and that, even if your work were much more laborious, you would make no less of an effort to please Him.

Offer Him your weariness in union with all that Jesus bore for your salvation.

If your work turns out well, bless Him Who grants you success; if it does not succeed, accept the humiliations He allows so that you may practice patience. If you bring God into all your actions, even those that seem smallest and most abject, they will be rendered sublime to the point of winning a higher degree of glory for you in heaven.

CHAPTER 24

LOVE OF JESUS

The Believer

HOLY Mother of Jesus, when you lived at Nazareth with the Savior, men did not know Him for what He was; therefore they looked down on Him. But He was content to be loved sincerely, ardently, tenderly, and constantly by His Mother.

Knowing His Divinity and infinite perfections, you loved Him more than all the angels and saints loved Him, love Him now, or will love Him in time to come.

Your love was superior to that of ordinary mothers, for in Him you loved a Son who was both God and Man. Therefore there was enkindled in you that immense desire to see Him loved by all rational creatures.

It is the mark of a pure love that it seeks to communicate itself and wants all hearts to be fired with its own spark.

We would have to know Jesus as you knew Him if we were to love Him as perfectly as you did.

To speak in a way worthy of that love, we would have to be able to read the feelings of your heart for Him Who was its object.

Open to us that heart that loves so perfectly; show us all the purity and tenderness, the liveliness and generosity, of the sentiments that inspired it.

Mary

My child, I would not have been worthy to be the Mother of Jesus if my love for Him had not been greater than that of all other intelligent creatures. That love daily grew greater in me because daily I discovered new perfections in this Divine Child.

I experienced no sweetness and happiness except in that love. It was my food, my life, my rest, my joy, my delight. I lived a poor and obscure life at Nazareth, but I was well rewarded by the treasure I possessed in the person of Jesus. Because of that possession alone we thought ourselves richer than the mightiest kings.

Happy, beyond telling happy, are those who live for love of Jesus, and who breathe only for Him! The love of Jesus makes them calm and content of heart, and nothing can long please them without that love. What pleasure, after all, can a man find in this world if he has not tasted the lovableness of Jesus? The more one loves, the greater the pleasure one finds in loving Him Who is truly infinitely worthy of being loved.

However greater your sufferings in this life, there is none equal to that of not loving Him. If a man does not love Jesus, has he really known what Jesus is? Jesus unites in Himself all natural perfections, but in so eminent a way that they make of Him the Creator's masterpiece.

He unites in Himself all the perfections of grace, in such a way that all men must come and share His fullness.

He unites in Himself all the perfections of the Divinity that dwells substantially in Him. He is powerful with the power of God, beautiful with the beauty of God, wise with the wisdom of God, holy with the holiness of God.

The Believer

Even if Jesus were not infinitely lovable in and for Himself, He would have become so by having infinitely loved me. What sufferings He endured to show me His love!

Mary

You must add, my child, that the immensity of His sufferings did not equal His desire for suffering. Love never says: Enough! But of all the loves that exist, the most ardent and the most eager to make itself known is the love of Jesus.

Jesus would have given even more than He did for your salvation if He could have given something more of Himself.

My child, if there is outside of Jesus an object more worthy of your love, He consents to your giving it, and if He deserves your love before and above everything else, will you dare refuse it to Him?

The Believer

How this world and all that is in it vanishes from before my eyes! I want to love, and I do love, naught but Jesus.

Mary

He who knows Jesus despises all else, and the world means nothing any longer to him who has tasted the sweetness of Jesus' love.

The Believer

I can, if I want, have Jesus for my friend. And if I neglect to obtain such a great blessing for myself, I deserve to be extremely unhappy.

Mary

My child, love Him Who cannot turn back on His promises or change His plans, Who is not subject to events outside Himself, and Who, far from being taken from you some day through death, will become in death your eternal possession.

Jesus is the only faithful and constant Friend Who does not fail when others abandon you.

A single word from this Friend brings consolation to the anxious heart, while all others are for the most part only the kind who console you when you have no need of it.

What repugnance or regret can you feel if the love of Jesus is in your heart? What enemy can harm you? If He rules and has His throne in your heart, you are the richest, most powerful, most fortunate man earth has seen or can see.

The love of Jesus is a blessing that needs no other to supplement it. For does Jesus not have the means of rewarding the heart that loves Him?

The Believer

My Jesus, my God, I ask you, by the love You have for Your holy Mother, grant me the grace so to love You that I will love no one else more, no one else as much as You, and that I shall do nothing except for Your sake.

I cannot love You as You deserve. But I want, with the help of Your grace, to love as much as I can and ought.

Enkindle in my heart all the love You want to receive from me. Let me burn with that Divine fire until it consumes me.

To know how lovable Jesus is and yet to be unable to love Him as He deserves is a torment that cannot be alleviated except by the ever renewed longing for a more ardent love.

CHAPTER 25

THE STUDY OF JESUS OUR MODEL

Mary

M Y CHILD, are you perhaps one of those Christians who talk a good deal more than they act? In moments of fervor your sentiments are splendid, but does your activity bear them out?

You tell God you love Him; it even seems that you do love Him, for when His grace makes itself felt in you, you shed sweet tears. But this is in fact no proof of true, sincere love.

The testimony to love that Jesus wants of you is that you should live your life according to the example of virtue He has given you.

The Believer

Mary, perfect model of every virtue, you sought to become ever more like Jesus during the years at Nazareth.

The Gospel tells us that you listened attentively to everything Jesus said and took careful note of all His actions. On these you meditated; and you *treasured all these words in her heart* (Lk 2:51).

Mary

Yes, my child, the study of Jesus was my chief occupation, the imitation of Him my main concern. Let your care, too, be to meditate on His life so that you may imitate it.

Turn all your attention to this. For there is no true knowledge except that which Jesus has. Let Him, then, be your only teacher.

Jesus is a King Who deserves all homage from you, and the principal honor He asks is that you imitate His virtues.

Compare yourself frequently to this great model, before the model Himself confronts you at the judgment seat of God.

The love Jesus has for you led Him to give you magnificent examples of humility, patience, and obedience. Imitate them for love of Him, and, when you find yourself in difficulty, think of all He has done for you.

Make it your aim to be, as far as possible, a faithful copy of Him in everything and at all times. When you pray, imagine to yourself His recollection during prayer; when you go to church, try to have His spirit of piety and sacrifice; when you speak to men, think of the modesty and meekness that marked His words.

If you want to imitate Jesus Who was *meek and humble of heart* (Mt 11:29), do not complain any more about your sufferings; return good for evil; flee this world's honors; love to be looked down on.

Christ never sought to please Himself (Rom 15:3); so too let God's glory and the accomplishment of His will be the source and goal of all your actions.

You know His inclinations and desires and sentiments. Now examine your own so that you may compare them with His and reform them. But bear in mind that such a reform, aimed at likeness to Jesus, cannot be done in a day.

Jesus is so perfect a model that you will never perfectly imitate Him. But every day of your life should be given over to the attempt to imitate some new aspect of that model.

And since you will never have the happiness of imitating Jesus unless the grace of Jesus helps you, ask Him for that grace every day of your life.

CHAPTER 26

THE HAPPINESS OF
A VIRTUOUS FAMILY

HEAVEN beheld a sight truly worthy of it when it gazed down on the Holy Family at Nazareth and Jesus living with Mary and Joseph. What tranquility and unity must have ruled in a home where every virtue dwelt and all unregulated passions were absent!

There, while Jesus *increased in wisdom and in age and in grace with God and men* (Lk 2:52), Mary kept her eyes fixed upon Him so that she might become like this model. Joseph was no less careful to profit by the example of the Mother and the Son. In this home everything was referred to God, everything done for Him. The simple presence of Jesus filled every heart with joy, and His Divine words set every heart on fire.

The submissiveness and obedience of Jesus filled Mary and Joseph with admiration and inspired in them a holy humility before God.

God of holiness, there You were indeed worshiped *in Spirit and truth* (Jn 4:24). How pleasing must have been the homage You received there!

No one can think of that Holy Family without envying it. How wonderful it would be if every Christian family took lessons in such a school!

If the love of God ruled in other families as it did under the humble roof that sheltered Jesus, Mary, and Joseph, they too would enjoy order, peace, and harmony.

Husband and wife would taste the innocent delights of marital union; children would be raised to fear God; servants would receive only example that was virtuous.

There would be none of the disastrous effects of jealousy and dissension between husband and wife, none of the scandals so frequent today. Prosperity would not lead to pomp and proud show, but would exercise a happy influence on the poor and would be sanctified by gratitude and Christian moderation.

A wise thrift would be respected, but the sordid hoarding inspired by avarice would be just as much shunned as the trappings of luxury. Adversity would not give rise to complaints and murmurings against God's providence, and He would be no less honored in time of need or simple sufficiency than in time of abundance or greatness.

The head of the family would exercise his authority without being imperious or arrogant; the wife would agree with the attitudes of her husband and would exercise great care over her household; both would have the consolation of seeing the growth of docile children who would in time walk the path of virtue.

From such families how much good would result for the whole society of the faithful! What lovable simplicity in way of life! What candor and innocence! What unity and love! What edification and marvelous fruits of holiness!

How calmly the days would pass! And when the time came to pay death the final tribute, we would willingly offer the sacrifice of our lives because we would have the consolation of having lived in holiness and love of God.

CHAPTER 27

EFFICACY OF PRAYER

WHILE Mary was at the wedding feast of Cana with Jesus and His disciples, the wine ran out. Mary was moved by the shame that the bride and groom felt, and, full of confidence in her Son's power, she told Him of their need.

God has always linked His graces to prayer. He is always ready to give those graces, but He invites us to ask for them, and He wants us to ask with confidence.

The lack of confidence is usually the sign of a weak faith. That explains why so many prayers are fruitless and unanswered.

When we want to offer God the homage of prayer, we need not wait for some favorable moment. Our God is always ready to hear us. He is constantly telling us: "*Ask, and you will receive; seek, and you will find*" (Mt 7:7).

We are the servants of a God Who is so kind that He can turn no one away and so rich that He gives to all. Why, then, are we so slow to ask graces for ourselves and, as Mary did, for others too?

Mary's prayer was brief; God, unlike men, does not require labored prayers of us. We need neither subtlety nor eloquence in dealing with Him. The prayer that pleases God and makes Him inclined to answer us is one marked by simplicity, in which we ask only what we think will be to His glory and our good, or at least what we know is not contrary to either. The sentiments of the heart, much more than fine words, win His favors.

The heartfelt sighs of Samuel's mother won for her not only the son for which she asked but also, in that son, a prophet and judge in Israel: *Hannah was praying in her heart* (1 Sam 1:13).

Jesus answered Mary in a way that gave no grounds for hope, yet she did not cease to hope, and she therefore obtained what she wanted.

Rarely shall we pray with perseverance and not be heard. Importunity displeases men and wearies them, but if you do not grow weary of praying to the Lord, He will not grow weary of hearing you.

No matter how fervent your prayer is, God seems to say to you, as He did to Mary, "*your hour has not yet come*" (cf. Jn 2:4). But if your confidence is truly unshakable, God will finally grant your request.

We only make ourselves unworthy of the Divine generosity when we decide to put a time limit He must meet.

It is true, of course, that despite our repeated prayers God sometimes does not give us what we ask of Him. But in such instances He gives us something we need far more than what we asked.

St. Paul asked to be freed of a temptation, but the assault went on. Since, however, he had prayed, God gave him a grace that enabled him to win great merit. Was he not heard?

You have been praying for many years to be rid of a bodily infirmity. God does not free you. But the patience to bear with the affliction has been given because of your prayer, and you have indeed been heard.

Frequently we think that we are asking God for something good, but it would be an evil for us if He were to grant it. He refuses it because He loves us.

We must distinguish between gifts of our sanctification and salvation and gifts that are purely temporal. The latter God gives even to His fiercest enemies, but the former He reserves for His chosen ones.

CHAPTER 28

VIRTUE IS COMPATIBLE WITH SOCIAL LIFE

CHARITY alone led Mary and her Son to be present at the wedding feast of Cana. Mary would undoubtedly have preferred to stay at home in Nazareth and enjoy the peace and sweetness of contemplation, but she did not want to sadden the newly married couple by refusing their invitation.

Virtue, therefore, is not incompatible with the social amenities; rather it makes it a duty to observe them, but to do so in a holy way.

If then you want to imitate Mary in every way, observe how she acted on such an occasion. What restraint in her speech, what modesty in her glances!

The prudence that marked her conduct is a lesson in the propriety and reserve that should be practiced even in recreation which is virtuous and innocent.

We must distinguish sharply between the laws of society and the laws of the world. Virtue does not acknowledge the latter except to do battle with them. It respects the former and observes them as far as possible, because they are not contrary to God's commandments. To abstain from all amusements would be, in a way, to do wrong to piety and to give substance to the false charge that virtue makes man a barbarian.

No, true virtue never makes a man unsociable. He can observe the laws of courtesy without being any the less devout.

On the contrary, true piety, because of its goal and motivation, can ennoble actions that are in themselves neutral.

Piety tells us: Do not give yourself wholly to any amusement, however innocent; it is enough for you to be present.

To avoid excessive distraction through amusements, try to recall from time to time the presence of God. Behave with the modesty and reserve you would show if Jesus and Mary were there with you.

Like the angel who accompanied Tobit, try to act like your friends, as long as they do nothing wrong, but at the same time, again like the angel, have an invisible food that will bring delight to your soul (cf. Tob 12:19).

Raise your thoughts to heaven. Think of the indescribable delights the saints enjoy, delights that are the reward for their indifference to earthly delights. Lift up your mind and heart to the Lord and tell Him that not all the pleasures of this world will have the power to make you forget the pure joys His service brings.

Tell Him that with the help of His grace you will, for the sake of a single glance from His love, gladly sacrifice all that could most please you in this life.

CHAPTER 29

LISTENING TO THE VOICE OF JESUS

DURING the thirty years at Nazareth Mary had enjoyed the presence of Jesus and the delight of learning from Him. It seemed that henceforth she had only to go over those lessons in silence and solitude without following Him to the various places He visited in His public life.

But St. John tells us: *"After this, He went down to Capernaum with His Mother, His brothers, and His disciples, and they remained there for a few days"* (Jn 2:12). During those few days Mary undoubtedly profited by His teaching.

The other evangelists tell us that on another occasion she could not get close to Jesus because of the crowd around Him that had gathered to hear His teaching, and so she sent word: *"Your Mother and Your brothers are standing outside. They want to speak with You"* (Mt 12:47).

No one knew better than she the value of these Divine lessons; no one felt more deeply the attraction of His conversation. How sweet it is indeed, for one who can distinguish the voice of Jesus from that of other men, to hear *the words of eternal life* (Jn 6:68) that come from His mouth!

A soul that has once tasted Jesus cannot live without Him. On countless occasions it has heard His voice, and it desires to hear it again and again. No place delights it if the beloved is not there; any voice displeases it if it be not His. How uninteresting such a soul finds the talk of men. For *they speak only of empty things* (Ps 119:85 — Vulgate), while the words of Jesus are *spirit and life* (Jn 6:63).

When such a person hears Jesus speak, he banishes all other thoughts and gives his whole attention to the Divine words, for these are far more pleasing than the greatest wonders one might hear on earth.

There is nothing he hears with greater joy, retains more faithfully, and reflects on more attentively; there is nothing that bears more abundant fruit in him.

If, like the bride in the Song of Songs, the soul sleeps, it also wakes, like the bride, at the least murmur of the bridegroom's voice. *I hear my beloved's voice. He is coming* (Song 2:8).

And the soul is not mistaken, for it knows Jesus' voice immediately, since it loves Him alone.

The world with its vanity and pleasures speaks a different language and the soul does not like to hear it. That language it knows only to reject it.

Magdalene did not recognize Jesus when He appeared to her after the resurrection, but as soon as He spoke, her heart knew that it was Jesus.

Jesus, my Savior, keep far from me all other voices, for they try so often to turn my attention from Your divine word. I want to hear no voice but Yours.

Empty amusements, frivolous things that have so often kept me from hearing Jesus' voice, I do not know you; leave me alone with Him.

That I may be fortunate enough to hear You, *Master, I will follow You wherever You go* (Mt 8:19).

When I can no longer hear Your voice at Nazareth, I shall go to Capernaum to hear it or to Jerusalem. Wherever I am, I can enjoy the happiness I desire. Speak, Lord! Speak always to my soul. *I will listen for God's response* (Ps 85:9).

Blessed is the man You admonish, O Lord, the man You teach by means of Your law, giving him respite in times of misfortune (Ps 94:12-13).

Your ministers often speak to me on Your behalf, and I enjoy reading the many books that tell me of You. But if at the same time You did not let me hear Your voice as well, what impression would these others make on me?

What they tell me is true and moves me, but if Your grace does not accompany their words, the truth is not inscribed in my soul and does not penetrate my heart.

Speak, for your servant is listening (1 Sam 3:10), heavenly spouse of my soul, and listen to my voice in turn. Speak to my heart, that my heart may speak to Yours.

Your words teach me more in a day than the wise men of this world can teach me in many years.

It is because of the knowledge gained from You that men who are ordinary in the world's eyes can speak wonderfully of Divine love and reach the heights where they contemplate Your greatest mysteries.

CHAPTER 30

DO NOT SEEK THE WORLD'S GLORY NOR MEN'S ESTEEM

The Believer

BLESSED Mother Mary, you surely rejoiced at the honors given your Son on various occasions during His life of preaching, but your joy was solely for His sake and not at all for yourself. You never prided yourself on being chosen as Mother of the man who stirred the admiration of the crowds by His wonderful miracles and sublime teaching. Unlike other mothers who openly boast of the merits of their children and want to share their children's glory, you followed Jesus from place to place simply in order to hear His teaching and not to have a share in the praise and blessings heaped on Him.

You always preserved a humble heart in the midst of all that was best suited to draw the eyes and homage of the world.

Thus you condemned the quest for the world's glory and the love and esteem of men, those ill-fated poisons that infect our every action.

Mary

It is true, my child; by the Lord's favor I always kept away from what you rightly call an ill-fated poison.

Glory belongs to God alone. What has the creature to boast about? All virtue comes from Him.

In choosing me to be Mother of the Messiah the Lord had already honored me. Was I now to look for the world's honors as well?

The man who seeks God alone sees nothing worthwhile outside of Him. The honors of this world and all that men esteem most highly seem to him empty and frivolous things.

My child, consult your faith, consult reason too, and you will no longer be desirous of praise and honor. Your ambitions will change, and you will want nothing but the glory God has in store for His saints.

If you are forgotten and no account is taken of you, you should not be saddened but filled with joy. For there is no safer way of reaching a high place in heaven than the way of humiliation when it is followed in a spirit of faith.

Let the world's followers, then, have all the empty titles and all the distinctions of which they are so proud. You should aspire to a glory that is more real and solid. Frequently ask God,

THE HOLY ROSARY

PRAYER BEFORE THE ROSARY

QUEEN of the Holy Rosary, you have deigned to come to Fatima to reveal to the three shepherd children the treasures of grace hidden in the Rosary. Inspire my heart with a sincere love of this devotion, in order that by meditating on the Mysteries of our Redemption which are recalled in it, I may be enriched with its fruits and obtain peace for the world, the conversion of sinners and of Russia, and the favor which I ask of you in this Rosary. *(Here mention your request.)* I ask it for the greater glory of God, for your own honor, and for the good of souls, especially for my own. Amen.

1. The Annunciation
For the love of humility.

The Five

Joyful

Mysteries

Said on Mondays and Saturdays [except during Lent], and the Sundays from Advent to Lent.

2. The Visitation
For charity toward my neighbor.

4. The Presentation
For the virtue of obedience.

3. The Nativity
For the spirit of poverty.

5. Finding in the Temple
For the virtue of piety.

The Five
Sorrowful
Mysteries

Said on Tuesdays and Fridays throughout the year, and every day from Ash Wednesday until Easter.

3. Crowning with Thorns
For moral courage.

1. Agony in the Garden
For true contrition.

4. Carrying of the Cross
For the virtue of patience.

2. Scourging at the Pillar
For the virtue of purity.

5. The Crucifixion
For final perseverance.

The Five
Glorious
Mysteries

1. The Resurrection
For the virtue of faith.

Said on Wednesdays [except during Lent], and the Sundays from Easter to Advent.

2. The Ascension
For the virtue of hope.

4. Assumption of the B.V.M.
For devotion to Mary.

3. Descent of the Holy Spirit
For love of God.

5. Crowning of the B.V.M.
For eternal happiness.

The Five

Luminous

Mysteries

Said on Thursdays [except during Lent].

3. Proclamation of the Kingdom
For seeking God's forgiveness.

1. The Baptism of Jesus
For living my Baptismal Promises.

4. The Transfiguration
Becoming a New Person in Christ.

2. Christ's Self-Manifestation at Cana
For doing whatever Jesus says.

5. Institution of the Eucharist
For active participation at Mass.

PRAYER AFTER THE ROSARY

O GOD, Whose, only-begotten Son, by His Life, Death, and Resurrection, has purchased for us the rewards of eternal life; grant, we beseech You, that, meditating upon these Mysteries of the Most Holy Rosary of the Blessed Virgin Mary, we may imitate what they contain and obtain what they promise, through the same Christ our Lord. Amen.

℣. May the divine assistance remain always with us. ℟. Amen.

℣. And may the souls of the faithful departed, through the mercy of God, rest in peace. ℟. Amen.

THE NEW LUMINOUS MYSTERIES

THE new Mysteries, i.e., Mysteries of Light or the Luminous Mysteries, suggested by Pope John Paul II, are intended to offer contemplation on important parts of Christ's Public Life in addition to the contemplation on His Childhood, His Sufferings, and His Risen Life offered by the traditional Mysteries.

The Pope assigned these new Mysteries to Thursday while transferring the Joyful Mysteries—normally said on that day—to Saturday because of the special Marian presence in them.

as David did, not to let your eyes become enamored of empty earthly things.

Many have destroyed themselves by making an idol of the world; do not imitate them; shrink from their example!

The Believer

Holy Virgin, I shall draw profit from your example and lessons. I want no glory but that which comes from imitating your virtues.

But my heart is weak and easily deceived. Help me to attain the constancy of soul I need if I am to rise above the scorn and treacherous allurements of the world.

CHAPTER 31

HELP YOUR NEIGHBOR LOVINGLY AND GENTLY

The Believer

VIRGIN, gentlest of all God's creatures, show me how you acted toward the many ungrateful people whom Jesus taught and for whom He worked great miracles. Thus I shall learn how to put up with the faults of my neighbor.

How often you witnessed the ingratitude and betrayal Jesus received in return for the good He did!

Yet your thoughts and feelings toward His enemies were, like His, only thoughts and feelings of peace. You detested sin, but you loved the sinner.

It was only the offense against God that moved you deeply; you let no complaint against these foolish men pass your lips, and you even took up their cause with Jesus.

You acted toward them as you now act, after so many years, toward me!

I am the most faithless and ungrateful of your servants, yet you treat me with kindness and win ever new favors from God for me. Mother of the God of peace, win for me the grace never again to distress any man by unkind words.

Your very name and image causes me to think mild thoughts. Obtain for me the virtue of gentleness and the spirit of peace, so that I may merit the glorious title of "child of God."

Mary

Yes, my child, I will pray for you, but you must correspond to the grace I obtain for you from the Lord. Grace does not do away with difficulties; it only helps us bear them.

I know your neighbor is often a burden to you because of his moods and silly ideas and strange behavior. But if you are obedient to grace it will teach you to overcome your repugnance and win great merit.

The occasions for practicing heroic virtue did not come every day even to the saints; yet because they patiently put up with the faults of their neighbors, each day added a new luster to their crown.

A Christian's life is a life of sacrifices; and a man's neighbor, with his faults, is constantly giving occasion for multiplying such sacrifices.

All men sin many times. They ought therefore make of us the means they have of expiating their sins. One of the most effective of these means is to put up with one's neighbor in a spirit of penance.

In addition, my child, every man has his faults. The most perfect man is simply the one who has fewer defects than anyone else.

You will find defects in your brothers, and they in you. Be not one of those who think they have no defects and by that very fact have the greatest defect of all.

Your brothers put up with you as you are; put up with them as they are.

In bearing with your neighbor, show the patience he needs in bearing with you and with the defects he cannot but observe in you.

You have long been wearing yourself out trying to improve yourself but your efforts until now have seen little success. How then can you claim to correct those of others as you wish?

All your complaints at the annoyances you must put up with from certain people who displease you are not helpful and certainly will, not bring about their correction.

In dealing with such annoyances the only course of action for you to take is to ask Jesus to help you in drawing profit from them, in testing yourself, and in gaining more solid virtues.

CHAPTER 32

SUBMISSION TO GOD'S WILL EVEN IN WHAT SEEMS CONTRARY TO HIS GLORY

The Believer

MOTHER of Jesus, what sorrow you felt at seeing the Jews draw such little profit from your Divine Son's preaching!

That heavenly teaching, although accredited by striking miracles, could not convert so many stubborn minds that preferred to blind themselves. Like sick men who push away the hand that wants to heal them, these unbelieving men rejected the salvation offered them.

What were your feelings then? You groaned at the blindness and stubbornness of these headstrong people, but you groaned in silence and never stopped praying God for their conversion.

Mary

My child, the thing I certainly wanted above all else was for Jesus to be known. My zeal for His glory made me feel deeply the hardening of Jewish hearts. Yet why should I have therefore lost my peace of soul?

I knew that God often makes use of evil in carrying out His plans; I knew He draws good from evil. Therefore in silence I adored the infinite wisdom that at times allows wickedness to triumph.

The Believer

Holy Virgin, that patience will be my model in all circumstances of life and especially in those in which my faith will feel itself shaken.

Mary

Yes, my child, when you see wickedness walking happily with head held high and trampling innocence down, do not let yourself be swept along by the impulses of an embittered zeal. True religious spirit forbids such a course.

Why can you not bear with what God Himself accepts? He could prevent what you regard as scandalous, but He does not do so and He has His reasons. It is for you to adore them.

Nothing happens in our world without His permission. And everything, evil as well as good, serves His providential purposes. It is not granted to you now to understand His plans but the day will come when you will recognize their full justice and wisdom.

You should not, of course, be insensible of the evils in the Church; it is only right that they should be a source of affliction for you; you may even weep bitterly over them, as God Himself does. But if you were to be scandalized at them so that your faith suffered or you lost your peace, that would not any longer be zeal but an abuse and an excess.

One true virtue does not destroy another.

Submission of mind to what God allows is compatible with genuine zeal for the glory of God.

Evils call for your tears and laments, but they should be tears shed at the Savior's feet and laments voiced to Him.

Tell Him of your anguish; ask Him to put an end to your afflictions; speak to Him with a holy freedom. He will not be offended.

Awake, O Lord. Why do You sleep? Rise up and do not abandon us forever. Why do You hide Your face and continue to ignore our misery and our sufferings? (Ps 44: 24-25).

It is on You that men dare declare war; it is Your holy name that is scorned, Your religion that is blasphemed, Your work that men seek to destroy! Defend Your cause. Do not let evil prevail any longer, for it is Your very glory that is at stake.

My child, if you address Him in this fashion, you will do justice to what zeal for God's glory and your religion requires, and you will be able to wait in peace for the Lord to come and console you.

CHAPTER 33

MARKS OF TRUE HOLINESS

ONE day a woman cried out to the Savior: *"Blessed is the womb that bore You and the breasts that nursed You!"* But Jesus answered her: *"Blessed, rather, are those who hear the word of God and obey it"* (Lk 11:27-28).

Here Jesus intended to tell us that what most distinguishes Mary is not her dignity as Mother of God but her constant fidelity to all her religious duties.

Her greatest merit does not consist in the prerogative of her maternity which came to her from God and from God alone, but her holiness which, while indeed requiring the grace of God, also was the fruit of her correspondence to grace and her cooperation.

What merits God's rewards is not what He does for us but what we do for Him.

The good servant of whom the Gospel speaks earns a reward not for having received the five talents but for having made them yield a profit.

You are proud, and rightly so, of that Divine sonship which you received in baptism. But remember that this dignity will not win you a place among the saints unless you accompany it with holiness of life.

Among the saints are some who had visions and ecstasies. But that is not why you should envy their lot.

The saints were people who were faithful, perseveringly faithful to the will of God, and that is what you must try to imitate in them. You have embraced a holy profession? But it is not in the holiness of the profession that you must find your security, but in your watchfulness and care in carrying out all your duties.

Judas, in all probability, worked miracles, but he was nonetheless rejected. We do not read that John the Baptist ever worked miracles; yet in the Gospel the Son of God bestows the highest praise on him.

Among men you can be esteemed even if your life is not a holy one; but with God a man is nothing if he is not a saint. And a man is not a saint if he does not do deeds that are holy.

This must be for us, as it was for Mary, the true basis of our dignity.

Understand, then, that God does not make your salvation depend on extraordinary gifts of nature or grace. Rather He has made you yourself the arbiter of your salvation by making it depend, under Him, on you.

O Lord, who may dwell in Your sanctuary? Who may abide on Your holy mountain? The one who leads a blameless life and does what is right (Ps 15:1-2).

STANDING BY THE CROSS

Mary stood silently near the Cross of her suffering Son and heard Him give her into John's care before He died. This made her our Mother also.

BOOK 3

*Life of the Blessed Virgin Mary
from the Death of Jesus
to His Ascension*

Chapter 1

THE LOVER OF JESUS MUST CLIMB CALVARY AND SUFFER WITH HIM

Mary

JESUS climbed Calvary. Come with me, my child, for He invites us to go up with Him; you may not desert Him.

Our love for Jesus would surely not be worthy of Him if we deserted Him in His sufferings, in that moment when everyone denied and insulted Him.

It is true enough that we cannot help Him, but at least we can share His suffering and unite our tears to His blood. We can give Him the comfort of seeing that we are ready to suffer, for love of Him, anything He permits.

The Believer

Noble Virgin, can we show Jesus true love only by following Him to Calvary and suffering with Him? Can we not also show our love in tranquility and peace?

Mary

In tranquility and peace, my child, it is easy to give proof of that love; but it must also be proved in pain and tears.

Jesus said: *"Whoever does not carry his own cross and follow Me cannot be My disciple"* (Lk 14:27).

You must therefore regard any day as a happy one on which you have occasion to endure something for love of Him.

Many Christians love the divine Giver solely for His gifts; they are like earthly friends who never love except for a return.

They claim to love Jesus with all their hearts, yet they have not the courage to *keep watch with* Him *for just one hour* in the garden of His agony (Mt 26:40).

They claim that they will follow Him *even to death* (Mt 26:35), but fear of suffering weakens love very quickly and they follow Him only *at a distance* (Lk 22:54).

My child, if you love Jesus, you must love His cross too, and if you love Him with all your heart, you must embrace with all your heart the crosses He sends you. Anyone who is not forced to carry Jesus' cross, as Simon of Cyrene was, but gladly shares the bitter gall given to Him on Calvary, truly loves Jesus. *For gold is tested in the fire and worthy men in the furnace of humiliation* (Sir 2:5).

Jesus lived amid tears; would you live amid delights?

The true Christian is a man like the patient Jesus, dying and dead on the cross.

If Jesus seems to you to have deserved any of your love for having suffered on your behalf, why should you not love the suffering Jesus sends you so that He may also give you a share in His glory?

Was it not necessary that the Messiah should suffer these things and enter into His glory? (Lk 24:26). There was no other way for me, just as there was no other way for the saints.

The Believer

Virgin Mother of God, you suffered so much pain, and you loved the pain because you loved Jesus. Intercede for me that I may overcome my weakness, my sensitivity, and the natural abhorrence I have for the cross. Let my heart, my mind, and all that is in me show that I love my God.

You were the holiest and the most afflicted of virgins. I want to share your sorrows, provided I can share your love.

Teach me to love the cross of Jesus and to find my delight in it, so that at the moment of my death the crucified Jesus may be my strength and consolation.

Mary

How can you trustingly embrace the crucifix at the moment of death, if you have in fact lived as an *enemy of the cross of Christ* (Phil 3:18)?

At the moment, far from lamenting that you have often been on the cross, you will wish you had always been there. My child, if you meet with insults, mistreatment, harsh persecution, misfortunes that seem insuperable, bear them all with persevering patience.

If I see in you an image of Jesus, my love for you will be intensified, for you will then be a son less unworthy of your mother.

The Believer

My mother, the motive that will inspire me henceforth and comfort me in all trials will be the thought that I am carrying my cross with Jesus and for Jesus' sake. But at the same time what a source of strength for me to realize that

my situation and dispositions will draw down
on me your special protection and love!

CHAPTER 2

CONFORMITY TO GOD'S WILL
IN SUFFERING

The Believer

I N MY present sad state I have recourse to
you, Consoler of the afflicted.

Inspire me with the sentiments that should
be mine in the evils I am suffering and in
those which still lie ahead of me.

Mary

My child, try to fill your heart with sentiments of full, entire, and perfect conformity to
God's will which rules and disposes of everything for His glory and your salvation.

When some affliction is close to you or
already upon you, when it stays with you and
even intensifies, or when it is followed by others, repeat frequently to God: *Yet not my will
but Yours be done* (Lk 22:42).

The thought of this Divine will was strong
in me and gave me comfort in the temple at
Jerusalem when Simeon told me: Jesus is *a
sign that will be opposed, . . . and you yourself
will be pierced with a sword* (Lk 2:34).

The thought strengthened and comforted me especially on Calvary when I saw Jesus nailed to the cross and breathing His last breath there in terrible pain.

As my love for Him knew no limits, neither did my suffering, but my resignation was as great as my pain and my love.

Banish from your soul, then, in time of adversity, every thought that cannot be expressed in these few words: *It is God's will.*

Any other thought will only increase your anguish and make you feel your unhappiness even more deeply.

How, my child, could you dare say you do not want affliction, when you realize that it is the Lord who sends it?

If a wise man wants only the good, what are we to think of God who is infinitely wise?

God hates the sin of those who contribute to your sufferings, but He intends to glorify Himself through the patience you show in bearing them.

He permits your enemies' sins, but wills the consequences which will sanctify you.

In Shimei David saw, not a subject who insulted him, but a just God Who made use of this lowly instrument to humble him and make him atone for his sins.

When Jesus spoke to His apostles of the cup
of His sufferings, He said nothing of the ingratitude of the Jews who were preparing that cup
for Him, but thought only of the will of His
Father Who was permitting this to happen.

In the Garden of Olives, Peter had not yet
learned that a Christian who is afflicted,
oppressed, and persecuted may take up only
the weapons of patience and submission. Jesus
said to him: "*Am I not to drink the cup that
the Father has given Me?*" (Jn 18:11).

My child, you are not denied the right to
ask God to deliver you from your afflictions,
but, if He still wants you to drink the cup of
suffering, say to Him: "*My Father, . . . let Your
will, not mine, be done*" (Mt 26:39).

Prayer

Pay no heed, Lord, to my great repugnance
for suffering. I want Your glory and the fulfillment of Your plans.

And if your sufferings increase instead of
lessening, say to Him: Yes, Father, I submit to
these new afflictions, because "*such has been
Your gracious will*" (Mt 11:26).

You will it, therefore I will it; You order it,
therefore I obey. If I must die, die I shall.

May the bitter blows You inflict on me and
allow others to inflict on me hasten the mo-

ment when I may enjoy the eternal sweetness of Your presence and Your love.

CHAPTER 3

PATIENCE

WHAT must have been the anguish of the Mother of the *Word made flesh* (Jn 1:14) when He became the Man of Sorrows and she saw Him handed over to the *power of darkness* (cf. Lk 22:53), dragged before tribunals, treated as a rabble-rouser, and struck by insolent soldiers! When she saw Him cruelly whipped, crowned with thorns, regarded as guiltier than Barabbas, weighed down by the cross, and sinking beneath the burden! When she heard the hammer blows that fixed the nails in the hands and feet of her beloved Son, and when she saw Him lifted up on the cross between two thieves and mocked by His enemies who were glad of His death and, when He grew thirsty, gave Him vinegar mixed with gall (cf. Jn 19:29) ! When she saw Him breathe His last on the cross and saw the witness given by the lance with which a soldier pierced His side to make sure that He was dead!

Throughout these fearful torments Mary gave proof of the most heroic patience. No one heard her utter the slightest groan.

On Calvary she imitated the silence of Jesus in the high priest's house where He was falsely accused, yet *remained silent* (Mt 26:63).

Soul in anguish, there is your model! When in your afflictions you must speak, speak, but speak with mildness and a tranquil spirit, and if you are not heard, suffer in silence, meeting injustice only with patience.

But with what kind of patience? A Christian patience that issues from the spirit of religion; not a purely human patience that is inspired by temperament and the thought of what is fitting.

Those who humble themselves under God's hand, adore His justice and mercy in the blows He gives them, and take as their model of patience Jesus and Mary—these are the true Christians who show you how you should suffer.

If you carry your cross impatiently, you only make it heavier, and add evil to evil.

The way of the cross is the way to heaven. That is why all the saints have traveled it. So now all the upright men on earth travel it; *many are the misfortunes of the just man* (Ps 34:20), because God is preparing a rich reward for his patience.

Unhappy are those Christians who turn to their own ruin what is intended for their salvation! They are like the thief at Christ's side on Calvary who blasphemed.

If we do not rebel against the Lord in our trials but we do complain about the crosses He sends us, then we deserve to have Him punish us by taking away this powerful means of sanctification.

We often implore heaven to free us of our crosses, but *we do not know what we are asking* (cf. Mt 20:22), for these crosses are a copious source of merit for us.

Where will you find greater fruits of holiness and surpassing virtue than in the shadow of the cross on Calvary?

Patience wins more merit for us in a few days than many years of a life entirely given over to works of devotion.

How often self-love creeps into these pious deeds! But in a life of suffering, the more we suffer, the greater our merit.

Let us not desire one cross more than another. Let us never say: "I will bear this cross more patiently than that."

Christian soul, any other cross than the one you have would not suit you better. God knows better than you do what you need. If you were to choose your own crosses, you would deceive yourself in making the choice. Whatever God bids you endure He suits to your need, your strength, and His plans for you.

CHAPTER 4

GREATER AFFLICTIONS FOR GOD'S MOST FAITHFUL SERVANTS

M Y GOD, for thirty-three years Mary always had a vivid image in her mind of the torments her Son was to suffer. Yet that was not enough: she had to be a witness of that death itself.

You did not wish Sarah to be present at the sacrifice which Abraham, at Your order, was to make of their son Isaac.

But I understand, Lord, that Mary, who was one day to be Queen of the saints, had to enter more deeply than all the saints together into the community of suffering that exists between Jesus and the elect.

I am not surprised, then, to see that many an upright man suffers greater afflictions as he becomes holier; rather do I see in this increase of suffering a sure sign of Your special love.

For what they do in order to please You, You reward them with afflictions that make them increasingly like the divine model they see on Calvary.

The persons whom You love best and who love You with a more ardent and tender love have found themselves closer to the cross on Calvary.

What a joy to be judged worthy of sharing Jesus' sufferings in a special degree!

A disciple is perfect when he becomes like his teacher (cf. Lk 6:40). Jesus, our teacher, whose perfections we must try to imitate, endured the greatest tribulations.

There are few perfect souls that have not been through some hard test.

They began to be virtuous; then You gave them the means of becoming perfect through adversity.

"*Because you were acceptable to God, you had to be tested by adversity,*" said Your angel to Tobiah (Tob 12:13).

In practicing the virtues which involve suffering we show God a more generous love than we do in the active virtues.

How consoling to be able to say with Peter: "*Lord, You know that I love You.*" (Jn 21:15) But we cannot understand what loving You really is until we have learned to suffer for You.

My God, great wrongs, imprisonments, or long cruel illnesses need not always be the lot of Your saints, but You have at least prepared other crosses for them which may not seem so terrible but which serve to make them die to themselves.

We do not know all the violent struggles to be undergone by souls You wish to purify and call to a high degree of holiness.

They may seem outwardly to be enviably, tranquil, but interiorly they must often wage a bitter war.

You do not provide the elements or evil men with arms against Your saints, but You do allow hell to rage against them so that they may be sanctified. The more they must struggle, the more perfect their virtue becomes.

Supreme Lord, by adoring Your will, their faith is strengthened and intensified as they submit in an ever more perfect way and acknowledge in You a wise Father Who *chastises every son whom He acknowledges* (Heb 12:6).

Their hope becomes ever more lively. They know Your infinite goodness; they are sure that, far from abandoning them to the wrath of their enemies, You will hasten to protect them; they take courage amid the conflict from the thought that the present burden of our trial *earns for us an incomparable weight of eternal glory* (2 Cor 4:17).

Their love becomes ever more intense. They are increasingly detached from creatures and live only for Him of Whom it is said: *God is the rock of my heart and my portion forever* (Ps 73:26).

Then, more than in any other situation, You are honored by their fidelity. In time of consolation men often serve You out of self-interest.

My God, in my sufferings I have often said that You no longer loved me. Henceforth I shall say: "I thank God, for this trial is a gift of His love."

His faithful servants and friends, the saints, endured sufferings much greater than mine, because they were more worthy of His concern and graces.

Let us suffer with the patience and resignation of the saints so that we may win the grace of suffering even more.

CHAPTER 5

OUR REPUGNANCE FOR SUFFERING SHOULD NOT SURPRISE US

The Believer

THE sight of the cross disturbs me deeply, holy Virgin, and I turn to you. I feel a very strong repugnance for suffering, and this attitude frightens me.

Mary

My child, natural repugnance is no fault in God's eyes. It makes it all the more meritorious for you to be perseveringly submissive to His will.

When people say the saints loved suffering, the meaning is not that they had any natural liking for it.

The man in them groaned at the thought; it was the Christian who rejoiced. Nature resisted, but the Christian triumphed over nature.

Do you perhaps think that my sensibilities were dulled on Calvary? If every mother feels keenly the evils that afflict her children, imagine my suffering at seeing my Jesus weighed down by so much infamy and torment.

You would have to have loved Jesus as I did to understand the immensity of my pain.

Even Jesus, in the Garden of Olives, allowed Himself to feel deeply the fear of suffering and death.

He did not allow His divinity, which gave infinite value to His suffering, to lessen His experience of it.

My child, if in affliction you sincerely want whatever God wants, you need not be at all disturbed by the repugnance you feel against your will.

Even if you find yourself yielding to natural feeling, do not lose heart; that would be to add a new fault to your lack of patience.

It is secret pride that makes you upset because you are not perfect. You are weak, and

God knows your weakness. You are a man, not an angel.

No man can live his entire life without committing some small faults, even though he tries to avoid them all.

Unlike me, you were not conceived in freedom from sin nor exempted from all inclination to evil and all the weaknesses proper to mankind.

When a complaint escapes you, promptly ask pardon of God. Promise Him you will do better. Ask His grace for this purpose, regain your tranquility, and increase your watchfulness over yourself.

You cannot better expiate a fault than by the humiliation it makes you feel.

My child, only with the saints in heaven will you be unable to sin.

The Believer

Queen of saints, when will that good fortune be mine? When shall I be freed of the fear of offending my God, that fear that is painful to a heart that loves Him?

Mother of grace and mercy, help your servant! Give me your powerful protection and be my shield against the enemies that seek to destroy me.

CHAPTER 6

THE CRUCIFIED JESUS INSPIRES US TO SUFFER WITH UNWEARYING COURAGE

The Believer

A T THE death of Jesus the earth shook, heaven was darkened, the rocks split, and all of nature was convulsed.

I admire you greatly in that moment of catastrophe, Mary, because you *stood near the cross of Jesus* (Jn 19:25) and offered anew at each moment the sacrifice Jesus was making to His eternal Father.

How could you bear such a sight? Where did you get such strength and courage?

Mary

I kept before my eyes a cogent model: Jesus crucified. He spoke only words of peace; He suffered with perfect resignation to His Father's will; He asked that His executioners might be pardoned through the merits of His sacrifice.

I watched Him carefully; I entered into His heart and tried to make all His sentiments my own.

As I saw Him give His life so generously for men amid the most fearful suffering, I learned to make the generous sacrifice of what was dearest to me in all the world: Jesus Himself.

My child, you find at the foot of the cross, as I did, comfort in bitter suffering, strength when you are beaten down, and courageous resignation in sacrifices God asks of you.

When you are afflicted, do not go looking to men for comfort; their compassion is barren and soon wearies.

After giving you their sympathy, they finally become bored by the narrative of your sufferings and, in the end, by your very presence.

Then you will be left to yourself and your thoughts, and you will find the burden of grief ever heavier to carry. The efforts you will make to pull out the arrow that wounds you will often serve only to push it deeper into your flesh.

In the hour of battle, my child, arm yourself with the image of Jesus on His cross. Let the crucifix be your first source of help on days of darkness and misfortune.

However slack your courage may be, you will find strength there. However strong the bitter taste in your heart, you will find consolation there.

Do you suffer because of what men do to you? Behold on the cross the most outraged of fathers, the most scorned of masters, the most abandoned of friends, the most persecuted of just men.

Do you suffer from hell's attacks? Contemplate Jesus on the cross as He is buffeted by hell's wrath.

Will you dare complain that heaven treats you too severely when you see the sternness of the heavenly Father toward His beloved Son?

To punish you for your sins God sends you some temporal trials; but what are these when compared to what Jesus suffered in order to rescue you from eternal punishment?

As you gaze at your crucifix, say: "I was redeemed by the extreme sufferings of God." It is only right that the redeemed soul should attain some likeness to its redeemer through suffering.

My child, if you cannot have the consolation of resembling Jesus in virtue, at least have the consolation (your crucifix will say to you) of resembling Him somewhat in suffering.

Have recourse to Him in every evil, anguish, and temptation.

Kiss your crucifix affectionately, bathe it in your tears, clasp it lovingly to your breast. Imagine that you are on Calvary and are allowed to embrace the feet of your God who is suffering and dying for you. Tell Him of your afflictions,

unite them to His, and ask Him to help you
find them easier to bear.

Ask this merciful Savior to let you hear
from His cross some strengthening words that
will help you endure your anguish of soul.

Tell Him you will not let Him go until He
has restored your peace and tranquility and
strengthened you with His grace.

If you are faithful to this holy exercise, your
tears will be dried up, you will have peace
again, courage will replace weakness, the cross
will no longer be so heavy for you, and bitterness will be changed into joy.

If you still have much to suffer, try to stir up
in yourself the patience, resignation, and love
which made the Apostle say: *"I rejoice when I
endure weaknesses, insults, hardships, persecutions, and distress for the sake of Christ"* (2
Cor 12:10).

CHAPTER 7

ATTITUDE TO ENEMIES

MARY could certainly have no greater enemies than the Pharisees and those other
Jews who conspired against her Son and caused
Him to be condemned to death. But she was
united in sentiment to Jesus who loved His enemies so much that He gave His life for their

salvation. Therefore, with the same love that Jesus had she said: *"Father, forgive them"* (Lk 23:34).

She saw these implacable enemies of Jesus boasting at the success of their crime. She heard the curses they heaped on Him and the blasphemies they poured out against Him.

Any other mother would have called down the vengeance of heaven against these wicked, sacrilegious men. But Mary had been trained in the school of the *God of peace* (Heb 13:20) and her heart was filled with entirely different thoughts.

Jesus on His cross addressed to God words of mercy for His persecutors and those who caused His death. At the foot of the cross Mary offered on their behalf the blood of the adorable victim they had immolated.

If the Jews could have seen in the hearts of Jesus and Mary the sentiments of tender love these two had for them, they might have been moved and might have repented.

From these two hearts, so full of anguish yet so overflowing with love, we must learn the spirit of love and forgiveness of enemies that the Gospel prescribes.

Jesus and Mary found their glory in pardoning offenses. Were they perhaps mistaken in what they thought true glory to be? Are we contemptible if we imitate these glorious models?

Can any injury done us be compared with the outrages inflicted on the Savior and His holy Mother?

Next to Jesus, Mary was the dearest object of God's love. The outrage inflicted on Jesus was infinite; that inflicted on Mary was the worst that could be conceived after that inflicted on her Son.

Yet with what love Jesus shed His blood and offered it to the Father to win grace for sinners! With what love Mary implored the Father to hear her prayers for them and the prayers that issued from her Son's blood!

Must not the most violent hatred die at the foot of that cross where we see Jesus and Mary so movingly interceding for those who raised up the cross?

The cross, which is the precious instrument of our salvation, will only hasten our damnation if we dare approach it with hatred in our hearts.

My God, the love of one's enemies is due to a special grace. I ask it of You through the merits of Jesus and Mary whose hearts were so gentle to the greatest ingrates, so loving toward the most impious persecutors.

Admirable and lovable hearts of Jesus and Mary, so good to all those who caused You such deep pain, fill my heart with Your generous sentiments.

Henceforth, whenever I feel the desire for revenge arising in me, I shall unite my heart in spirit to these sacred hearts, and I shall keep it thus united until it is full of those sentiments of goodness, love, mildness, and forgiveness with which theirs are full.

CHAPTER 8

THE SUFFERING OF RELATIVES AND FRIENDS

AT TIMES God afflicts us in the person of relatives and friends, and our affection for them makes us feel their sufferings deeply.

What anguish for a mother to see her son on a bed of pain, or for a friend to see fearful trials weighing on a friend and be unable to help him!

The anguish is frightful and not to be reproached as long as it is subordinate to God's will. It becomes reprehensible when it ceases to be resigned and breaks out into complaints against divine providence.

Imagine the suffering of Mary during the passion of her Son who had shown her such tender and incomparable love!

How often she must have said in her heart: "*My Son, my Son! If only I had died instead of You, my Son, my Son!*" (2 Sam 19:1).

If the daughters of Zion wept as they saw Jesus passing by weighed down by the cross, who can imagine the anguish of Mary as she saw Him on the altar of pain, agonizing and breathing His last? If only she could have brought Him some relief, or held His thorn-crowned head, or moistened His thirst-dried lips, or suffered for Him! But no, she had to stand there and simply look on at all His torment and hear around her the sacrilegious voices that insulted the very power and Divinity of Jesus.

There is a sweetness in suffering for someone we love. How hard it is to see someone we love suffer and be unable to console him!

What then was Mary to do in such a terrible difficulty? Was she to endure to the end the horrible sight or go away and spare herself the pain of seeing her Son die amid torments?

Unlike the mother of Ishmael who chose to abandon her child so as not to have to see him die, Mary stayed by the cross, submitting peacefully to the decrees of the eternal Father and offering the sufferings of Jesus to Him for the salvation of the world.

She stayed because God wanted her to, and she stayed until the sacrifice was complete.

Her faith, submission, and love of God made her a second victim which heaven accepted with gratitude along with the holocaust offered by the redeemer of mankind.

Whoever you are—loving father or faithful friend, child or spouse, anyone about to lose the person who is your consolation in this world—learn to master your sorrow. Remember that if you fear losing a great deal on earth, you are in a position to gain much in heaven.

Our religion does not condemn your tears or your sensibility, but if you listen to it, it will teach you to govern and sanctify your tears and your feelings. It forbids you to abandon yourself to the deadly sorrow that refuses to be comforted, but it offers you the fulfillment of God's will as the motive best suited to console you.

Seek consolation for your weeping heart, but turn to God as well; adore His intentions and submit humbly to them. Try to alleviate the sufferings of people dear to you, for God would have you do so. He also allows you to ask for their healing. But ask with submission, leaving everything to Him. You can say to Him: "*O Lord, all my longing is known to You, and my sighs are not hidden from You. My heart throbs, and my strength is spent; even the light has faded from my eyes*" (Ps 38:10-11). Lord, my God, in You I trust, in You I hope; hear my prayer for this person's health. I am ready to do Your will, for I want whatever You want, my God.

CHAPTER 9

HOW TO BEAR THE LOSS OF DEAR ONES

JESUS was dead. How long the time must have seemed for Mary between His death and His resurrection! Jesus was dead. Mary had lost the most loved and lovable of sons.

David's sadness at the death of Absalom (2 Sam 19:1) and the cries of Rachel mourning for her children (Mt 2:18) express but weakly the sorrow of Mary now that Jesus was gone and she could no longer hear His voice. But in losing Jesus this holiest and most devout of mothers lost nothing of her virtue. Her faith in the prompt resurrection of her Son and her resignation to what God had ordained for His glory and the world's salvation were her support and consolation.

All you whom God has afflicted by taking what you most feared to lose—mother desolated by the death of a dearly loved son, weeping wife who sees yourself prematurely condemn-

ed to a sad widowhood—do not lose sight of
the model now set before you.

Your tears are deserved. Joseph wept at the
grave of Jacob his father; Augustine wept at the
death of his mother Monica. But learn from
Mary to offer God the sacrifice of your sorrow;
learn from her how to bear the loss.

Death irreparably cuts the bonds that now
unite you to the person you mourn. But have
you lost all hope of being reunited? Are you
yourself to remain forever in this world? Does
your faith not teach you that true believers will
be reunited in God's bosom in a more perfect
union than they could ever have had on earth?

We shall rise up some day (cf. 1 Cor 15).
What a sweet and priceless hope the Apostle
offered the first Christians as a means of dry-
ing their tears and making them bear peacefully the loss of their brothers and sisters!

*You should not grieve as do those who have
no hope* (1 Thes 4:13). But weep as a Christian
who is full of faith, and, after you have given
expression to natural tenderness, bow your
head to God's will.

Only our holy, divine religion can provide
resignation and comfort.

Moreover, was this person whom you loved
so dearly and whom death has taken from you
your whole happiness on earth? Did you love

him more than you loved God who has allowed this separation for reasons before which you should bow down in adoration?

This person was dear to you; but God's will ought to be much dearer to your heart.

Perhaps your love for this person was not well ordered. Perhaps it was an excessive love, and the bitter, copious tears that refuse to stop are an evident proof of it.

Perhaps the person was a great obstacle to your perfection, and in taking him away God has been merciful to you both.

Learn from the affliction not to become attached to any creature. Set your whole affection on Him Whose *years have no end* (Heb 1:12). Or, if you love someone along with God, love him only because God allows you to love him or because He wants you to love him.

Then the love you owe to Jesus will suffer no diminution. Love God in the other person.

If you love in this way, you will always be ready, despite natural repugnance and feeling, to accept separation, when God wills it, from the legitimate object of your love.

On the day of the sacrifice your heart will undoubtedly groan and the tears will spring from your eyes. But you will also will what God wills; and this unity of wills shall put an end to your tears and sighs.

CHAPTER 10

FAITH AND HOPE IN TRIALS

THE Apostles had acknowledged Jesus to be *the Son of the living God* (Mt 16:16). Yet when it was time for Christ to suffer, they failed to live up to their faith; they hid it *and fled* (Mt 26:56).

Not so Mary, She followed Jesus right up to Calvary where she acknowledged Him as her redeemer and waited with sure hope for His resurrection, for He had said that He would rise.

After Jesus' death the disciples—those at least of whom St. Luke speaks—had but a small shred of hope that Jesus' prophecy would be fulfilled. But Mary, her soul free of any disturbance, persevered in her firm belief and hope that Jesus, Whom she had seen die a shameful death, would rise in glory and make the world accept His gospel message.

Mary's faith, so firm in its principles and so strong in time of trials, must be the model for your faith in every circumstance.

Impious men, of whom the world is full, may not give you the opportunity to declare your faith openly, but the enemy of your salvation will at least try to weaken it with doubts against revealed truth.

You must *resist him and be firm in your faith* (1 Pet 5:9), and do it courageously, without examining his suggestions. Then *he will flee from you* (Jas 4:7).

Immediately reject before the God of truth any doubt that rises in your mind. Such a prompt, generous, and heartfelt rejection will deepen and strengthen your faith.

It is especially in time of great trial that the devil seeks to cloud your mind and make you doubt the justice and wisdom, the power and goodness of the God who afflicts you.

At that moment recall what God says to you in the Sacred Scriptures about the necessity of suffering, the glory that follows upon it, and His plans in allowing men, and especially His most faithful servants, to be afflicted.

"I, the Lord, do not change" (Mal 3:6). What God once says is always true. His word is as immutable as He Himself is.

Whatever temptation, sorrow, bitterness, dryness, or desolation may be inflicted on you, take as your model the generous, persevering hope of Mary.

Then your soul, far from weakening and letting itself be beaten down, will find support in that virtue that is based on God's fidelity to His promises.

Hope against hope . . . and be fully persuaded that God can do whatever He has promised (Rom 4:18, 21).

He is your creator and has told you that He will not abandon the work of His hands but will watch over you. He is the supreme master of all nature; nothing is impossible or even difficult for Him.

The Lord always sustains His servants. They can have no doubts when they reflect on the promises of His covenant.

However unpleasant and painful your situation, you must base your hope on God's infinite providence, goodness, and power.

How often the Lord tells us, through His Prophets and Apostles, that He hears, supports, protects, and saves all who trust in Him!

Therefore, confidently ask His help, and never doubt that His mercy can relieve you of the unhappiness that now possesses you.

He permits us at times to be afflicted by terrible misfortunes so that we may learn better the power of lively hope in Him and experience His fatherly love.

Virtue greatly tested is far more profitable than tender devotion.

CHAPTER 11

CONSOLATION FOLLOWS TRIALS, BUT WE MUST LEARN TO SUFFER WITHOUT CONSOLATION

The Believer

Q UEEN *of heaven, rejoice, for the Son you bore in your womb and Whose death caused you so much grief, has risen as He promised* (Liturgy).

You enjoyed peace and intimate converse with Him until the day of His ascension into heaven.

It was only right that you more than anyone else should share the blessings of His resurrection, for you more than anyone else share His suffering and shame.

What joy and indescribable contentment you experienced in beholding His full splendor and glory!

Now indeed your tears were dried, the deep wound in your heart was healed, and your sufferings were over.

Mary

My child, *God is with His friends in their trials* (Ps 91:15) to strengthen them with His grace and, when it pleases Him, to make consolation follow on suffering, sweetness on bitterness. David had this experience: *When my anxious thoughts multiply within me, Your comfort fills my soul with joy* (Ps 94:19). The Lord at times lets the just man be afflicted but then He restores his tranquility.

The Believer

Holy Virgin, you know the trials that have long afflicted me; I am continually deprived of all consolation.

Mary

My child, if you have no sensible consolations, then acquire those of the spirit.

Is it not a wonderful consolation to realize that trials make you like Jesus and put you on the path to heaven?

God has His reasons when He allows His servants to suffer and does not give them the consolation of which you speak.

There have been many saints who have had to cross arid deserts and never taste a single drop of that dew.

The friends of Jesus should not be like earthly friends who are not willing to endure anything for their friends, unless they hope to be quickly recompensed.

Trust yourself entirely to providence; then when consolations become necessary or useful, you will be given them.

In your afflictions you have the grace of Jesus to sustain you. *My grace is sufficient for you* (2 Cor 12:9).

The saints whom Jesus allowed to suffer without sensible consolations found their consolation in the fact of having none, for they realized that their love was becoming nobler and purer.

Wait a while longer; wait for the promises of Jesus to those who suffer to be fulfilled. He is making ready for you in heaven an abundance of delights and blessings.

Enter into yourself, look into your own conscience, and consider whether your sins have not deserved the deprivation of all consolation.

For a repentant sinner it ought to be a genuine consolation to think that by suffering without consolation he is more surely expiating his sins.

CHAPTER 12

OUR AFFECTIONS SHOULD BE SET ON HEAVEN

MY SAVIOR, from the moment You left our visible world, all of Your holy Mother's thoughts, cares, affections, and sighs were concentrated on heaven.

She envied the lot of the angels and saints who rejoiced to have their beloved with them, and she asked them to tell Him how much she was suffering (cf. Song 5:8).

What more could the world offer her that might please her? She loved Jesus alone and wanted only Him.

Anyone who in this life makes Your grace and friendship his treasure knows but one sorrow: to be deprived of Your presence and divine embrace.

While waiting for death which alone can end my deprivation, I shall constantly direct to You, my Jesus, as Mary did, the fervent longings of a heart that wants You, loves You, seeks You, and finds Your coming always too long delayed.

Who will give me the wings of a dove? I shall take flight and come to rest at His side (cf. Ps 55:7-9)!

Shall this joy be long in coming? Will the bridegroom of my soul delay to tell me: " '*I am coming soon*' (Rev 22:20) to put an end to your wretchedness"?

"Come," says the bride. Her groans and sighs say continually: "*Amen! Come, Lord Jesus!*" (Rev 22:20). "*Of You my heart speaks; You my glance seeks; Your presence, O Lord, I seek*" (Ps 27:8).

I know I am made for greatness, yet I crawl along like a worm in this life. My Jesus, I am made for You, to possess You eternally.

Inexhaustible treasure, all is lacking if You are lacking. Light and brilliance are but darkness without Jesus.

Though you were to possess all created things, you would still be poor and unhappy if you could not say: "Jesus is my all."

Jesus is my all! The words say everything and contain everything. They are words understandable to one who loves Jesus above all else.

Far, then, from my heart be every other love.

Jesus, by Your grace inflame me ever more completely with the fire of Your love. Let that divine fire burn and consume me.

If I am not allowed to see You soon, my Savior, I shall try to make up for it by loving You.

My love, which founds my hope of seeing You some day, will be my consolation as long as my exile lasts.

CHAPTER 13

HOW TO DRAW THE HOLY SPIRIT TO US

JESUS had promised His disciples that He would send the Holy Spirit; to make ready to receive Him, Mary withdrew to the upper room with the apostles and other disciples of Jesus.

In silence, recollection, and practices of piety they prepared to receive the Spirit Sanctifier. All were gathered in one place, all were of one heart and will; they poured out ardent prayers that the Spirit might descend on them. Such are the dispositions required for receiving the God of love. He will communicate Himself to fervent souls who seek Him apart from the noise and tumult, and utter ardent and heartfelt prayers.

How effectively Mary hastened the coming of the divine Spirit by her fervent prayers, her pure desires, her solicitous love!

All who were filled with the same expectation must have felt greatly inspired by the presence and example of the Blessed Virgin.

She was already full of grace, but the Holy Spirit, desiring to enrich His bride still further with His gifts, created in her all the dispositions He wanted her to have.

The more a soul is under the influence of the Holy Spirit, the more numerous the further gifts it can obtain from Him.

Because a soul is faithful, it has already received many graces; but if it perseveres in fidelity, it will receive still more, for the treasury of God's graces is inexhaustible.

Anyone who knows, as Mary did, the excellence of these gifts will find nothing any longer worthwhile on earth. God's gifts will be the sole object of his desires.

What are we to think of the indifference of most Christians in this respect and of their lack of ardent desire for what is worthiest of their ambitions?

Are they equally indifferent to the world's favors? Far from it! No trouble is too much to obtain them, no means is left unused.

They regard the lack of worldly goods as shameful, but they do not blush for their spiritual poverty.

Divine Spirit, source of every grace and every gift, You alone can give me true riches.

I acknowledge with lively regret that my infidelity to Your inspirations has made me wholly unworthy of Your benefits.

But I unite my heartfelt prayers to those Mary offered You in the upper room.

Thus united, my prayers will be more acceptable to You and will draw Your favor to me.

I humbly implore this holy Virgin, who is so influential with You, to intercede for me.

Virgin, spouse of the Holy Spirit, obtain for me the spirit of wisdom, so that I may taste the riches of heaven and find tasteless all the deceitful goods and empty riches of this world.

Obtain for me the spirit of understanding and light that I may be enlightened here in this realm of darkness and come to know the ways of God and the truths of eternity.

Obtain for me the spirit of discernment and counsel so that I may discover and avoid the snares which the enemies of salvation and perfection have laid for me.

Obtain for me the spirit of strength and courage that will raise me above my weakness, enable me to overcome my passions, resist the world's vanity, and strengthen myself against my own inconstant heart.

Obtain for me the spirit of piety and fear of the Lord that will guide and inspire me in His service, in the observance of His law, and in the worship I owe Him as my creator, father, savior, and judge.

CHAPTER 14

ZEAL FOR GOD'S GLORY AND THE SALVATION OF SOULS

The Believer

HOLY Virgin, I love to think of you amid the little flock of faithful servants who gathered around you after the ascension of Jesus and the descent of the Holy Spirit; it was the efforts and preaching of the apostles that brought them there.

JESUS LIES IN MARY'S ARMS

The friends of Jesus took Him down from the Cross and laid Him in the waiting arms of His sorrowful Mother. Then the body of Jesus was placed in a tomb near Calvary.

In you they had a most tender and zealous mother. Who can say how much you did for the young Church of Jerusalem?

When the apostles set out to win the world for Christ, your prayers went with them everywhere, helping to support them in their labors and to overcome all obstacles and dangers.

In order to preserve the faith and virtues of the believers among whom you lived, you zealously tried to win their confidence. How could you but obtain it from all who were fortunate enough to be near you?

They could never sufficiently admire the affection Jesus' mother had for them, the free and ready access they had to you, and your respect for them.

If your high dignity, your virtue, and the enlightenment the Holy Spirit gave you won everyone's respect, your great goodness drew all hearts.

A mere glance at an afflicted person sufficed to make all his troubles easier to bear.

Your words, burning with a heavenly fire and endowed with heavenly power, softened the hardest hearts, inflamed the most lukewarm, encouraged the most timid, and gave new ardor to the most fervent.

If your zealous soul was grieved by the persecutions the Christians of Jerusalem had to bear, it could also find consolation in the progress the apostles were making among the gentiles: especially that of St. John before your very eyes at Ephesus where you found refuge in his home for some years.

You found great joy in that progress, for everything that contributed to the glory of your God's Church was of highest concern to you.

Queen of the apostles, obtain for me but a single spark of the sacred fire that consumed you for the glory of Jesus. Obtain for me, too, the grace to make others honor and love Him.

Mary

My child, how pleased I am with your desires! For zeal for God's glory must always mark the true Christian.

It is as necessary for a Christian as the love from which it springs.

Many consider it a mark of apostolic men alone; in fact, however, it must characterize every state. All Christians are obliged to win hearts to God through good example and appropriate advice, through words of comfort to the afflicted, and, above all, through prayer.

Frequently the conversion of a sinner is due to the sighs a zealous soul, unknown to the world, raises to God in solitude.

At certain moments of fervor you long to be among the pagans and to be toiling for their conversion. Holy desires, yes, but necessarily ineffective! You are looking far off for something quite near you.

Your duty is to glorify God by consoling the poor, instructing the ignorant, raising your children as pious Christians, fulfilling the obligations of your state, and leading others to fulfill theirs.

Think of your neighbor's salvation and bear always in mind that for his sake Jesus gave His life.

Many Christians will be punished for having neglected the good they could have done and for not having prevented the sins of others when they could have.

If you love the Lord, my child, you cannot better prove your love than by making others bless and love Him.

God has so few good servants! Give Him the joy, not only of being glorified in you, but also of seeing you use all the means your circumstances offer to glorify Him.

CHAPTER 15

CONSOLATIONS OF SPIRITUAL SUFFERINGS

The Believer

WHERE did you find strength, holy Mother of God, during the persecutions the early

Church had to endure, persecutions that touched even you?

Mary

My child, I found my consolation, as do all persecuted believers, in the remembrance of Jesus' sufferings, for the glory of His resurrection and ascension could not make me forget them.

I visited the holy places where the mysteries of redemption were effected, and especially Calvary where I meditated on Jesus' power and goodness and on the senselessness and ingratitude of men who had put Him to death on the cross.

When I remembered the cruelty with which men had treated Him, could I promise myself a peaceful and tranquil existence? Could I even want such a life?

You too, my child, should think often of how the world treated your Savior. In this thought you will find strength amid the afflictions you must suffer at the world's hands because you are faithful to God.

Jesus, for love of you, lived a difficult and toilsome life; for love of you He accepted contempt, outrage, and persecution. Now He calls you to be among His chosen ones; now you too must suffer, for love of Him.

If your virtues had not met with opposition and contempt from the world, they would not be true virtues.

All servants of God are dear to heaven, but the world hates them.

Strengthen yourself frequently by saying: "A *servant is not greater than his master. If they have persecuted me, they will persecute you*" (Jn 15:20).

I suffered as Jesus did and with Jesus. He was my model, my strength and my reward.

The Believer

Yet another trial, Queen of the saints, a trial greater than any borne by the other saints, was reserved for you. For you yearned with a great longing to be reunited to your Son, Jesus, in heaven.

Jesus reigned in glory but you were still in exile. To live on and to be separated from the one wholly deserving object of your tender love must have been for you a continual death.

But you knew how to obtain the consolations that would alleviate your sorrow. Every day you received Jesus in Holy Communion.

St. Luke tells us that the faithful *devoted themselves . . . to the breaking of bread* (Acts 2:42), and we are sure that you who loved Jesus more than anyone else received His adorable body and blood each day.

Mary

Yes, my child, it was in my daily communions that I found new strength each day to bear my long sad exile.

O those sweet hours when I could possess once again within me the Jesus with Whom I had lived for so many years!

In those happy moments I prayed with daily increasing ardor that my soul's beloved would take me *into His chambers* (Song 1:4). I begged Him to hasten the moment when I would possess Him again without any veil between us and enjoy forever His blessed presence.

But I also adored the divine will and submitted my desires to it. Communion was my joy and strength in the continuing struggles I had to endure, for it raised me to heaven and accustomed me to obeying ever more perfectly Him Who loved me so much and declared that He was my all.

A son who truly loves his father surely wants to be always with him.

A Christian who truly loves Jesus would gladly surrender all he holds precious in this world if he might go and be united to Him in heaven.

Here, far off from God, he suffers and sighs, until I *in my righteousness shall see Your face; when I awaken, I will be blessed by beholding You* (Ps 17:15).

He cries out with the prophet: *"How long will You hide Your face from me?"* (Ps 13:2).

But he finds relief from his anguish in submission; he learns that Jesus lived on earth in order to carry out His Father's will; he seeks Jesus in the Blessed Sacrament as often as he can; he hopes and trusts that Jesus will soon take him to Himself in heaven.

Under the Eucharistic veil his beloved, who is present as really as He is in heaven, visits him and speaks to him, and their hearts are united in the closest union.

Yet a while, and the veil will be lifted; and Jesus Christ will show Himself *as He is* (1 Jn 3:2) in all His splendor.

CHAPTER 16

PREPARATION FOR DEATH

THE entire life of the Blessed Virgin was a constant preparation for death.

What great and extensive merits she must have accumulated in a life of sixty years or more that was spent entirely in the practice of love of God!

That love increased in her at every moment and was so perfect at the moment of her death that death itself must be attributed to a violent outburst of love rather than to any weakening of nature.

Imitate the Blessed Virgin by consecrating to God each moment of a life which He gave you, not that you might become rich on earth or honored, esteemed, and applauded, but that you might serve Him and in His service win the crown of immortality.

Even if you possessed all the world's wealth and ruled all its peoples, what would remain of that after death?

You must leave everything behind, and everything must abandon you.

After death, the only possession you have left is the good things you did for the Lord in this life.

Learn wisdom from the example of those Christians who think of death only at the end of their lives and die with the vehement regret that they gave only a few days, perhaps only a few hours, to the important matter of their salvation, whereas it is not at all too much to devote a lifetime to it.

The number of fools is infinite (Eccl 1:15), Sacred Scripture tells us.

Most men are like the man who only thinks of making preparations for a journey when the moment of departure has come, or like the criminal who during his trial insults the judge and is still making plans for amusements as he is being led to the gallows.

If you are not to become attached to this life, you must think often of the eternity that follows it.

Many avoid thinking of death because they fear it. But the way to learn not to fear it is to think of it and constantly prepare for it.

A holy life makes it easier to think of death, and the thought of death contributes to a holy life.

Consider that what yesterday gave you joy may in death be a reason for punishment. To have consolation at the moment of death you must live virtuously.

If you had to die today or tomorrow, would you be prepared to face your judge? What penance have you done? What merits have you acquired?

Profit by the days left to you. If you cannot call back the past, you can at least make up for the waste of it. Only God can lengthen a life. Therefore you do not know whether you will live a long time or die shortly. But you do know, as the Lord tells you, that you will die at a time you did not expect.

If you may die at any moment, then you must at every moment be prepared to do so and must seriously consider that death is the moment that decides a whole eternity.

Pray the Queen of heaven to thank God for you for the time He has still given you to prepare for death. Ask her to obtain for you the grace to use the time in a holy way. To use it thus you must do each action as though it were the final action of your life.

A man dies a holy death if he dies as a man of faith, hope, and love. Make frequent acts of these virtues in the course of your life, and they will be your principal preparation for death.

Remember too that it is difficult for people to make acts of these virtues at the moment of death if they have not acquired the habit of doing so during life.

CHAPTER 17

HAPPY THE DEATH OF THE JUST MAN

The Believer

MARY, we would have to comprehend the love Jesus had for you, if we were to have any idea of the indescribable joy He poured into your soul at the moment of death. And we would have to comprehend your love for Jesus, if we were to have any idea of the immense yearning of your holy soul as you approached the happy moment that would unite you once again to the sole object of your love.

You drew your last breath in great peace, as though you were falling into a sweet sleep.

How could a virgin who had belonged to God alone be afraid at the moment of death? How could a person who had never sought consolation and happiness save in God, who had never had any ambition but to become ever more acceptable to Him, be fearful in that hour?

Mary

My child, if you want to experience the jubilation and sweetness of dying that were mine, then do not base your happiness on this world's goods or pleasures.

May I die the death of the just! (Num 23:10). That is the prayer of every Christian. Yet few share the detachment and scorn of the just for this world's goods. Most Christians, though made for heaven, think only of earth. What hope, then, will they have of entering heaven when the day comes to leave the earth behind?

Jesus shares His happiness with those who have loved Him greatly in this life.

Consoling indeed is the state of the man whose conscience is at peace when he comes to the end of a life full of temptation and suffering.

The dying sinner sees in Jesus only the pitiless judge, but the just man sees in Him a kind and merciful father.

During his life the just man too has sinned, perhaps seriously, perhaps often, but he has not waited for the hour of death to repent.

He has hope of God's mercy because he is ready to sacrifice his life with something of the generosity with which Jesus sacrificed His on the cross.

Since the day when he dedicated himself wholly to God, he has perseveringly struggled to be faithful to Him.

What then should he look forward to if not the crown of justice? How sweet it will be for you, my child, if, when you see death coming, you can say: *"I am leaving the world to go to the Father* (Jn 16:28); I am going to take possession of the inheritance He has stored up for me!"

I have glorified You on earth by finishing the work that You entrusted to me. So now, Father, glorify me in Your presence (Jn 17:4-5). Give me a share in the glory You promised me!

The man who has his lamp trimmed and ready is not afraid to hear the words: *"The bridegroom is coming; go out to meet Him!"* (Mt 25:6).

A holy person said on his deathbed: "I never thought it could be so sweet to die."

It is especially at the hour of death that Jesus shows those who love Him how very lovable He is.

When Jesus Christ has been the sole object of a heart's desire during this life, He does not allow such a heart to go astray in the hour of death. Rather does He make it by His grace resemble a torch that leaps up into new flame just as it seemed to be going out.

Love sincerely while you live and you will love ardently when you die.

The Believer

The most precious grace I can ask for and obtain from God's goodness, dear Mother, is the grace of dying with sentiments like yours.

You had lived in love, by love, and for love. Then you died of love! How the heart of the just man is inflamed by the thought of such a death! What more could I desire than to die such a death? But a sinner like me may not readily promise himself that kind of death.

Mary, at least obtain for me from Jesus, who is filled with love for me, the grace to have some little share in this death through love.

How wonderful to die loving Jesus, so that one's final breath is a sigh of love!

My Jesus, My Savior and my God, grant me that favor. I ask it of You because of the immense love of Your adorable heart for me and the immense love Your holy Mother has for You.

CHAPTER 18

HOLY LONGING FOR DEATH

The Believer

HOLY Virgin, the whole time you remained on earth after the ascension of Jesus was a time of sighs and affliction for you. You were being gradually consumed in the pure flame of divine love, and you wanted the end to come quickly.

I am too earthly to be able to imagine that state of holy longing that grew ever more intense down to the last moment of your life.

If I find it hard to understand David's suffering as he saw his exile prolonged, and the Apostle's when he so earnestly desired to be *freed from this life* (Phil 1:23), how can I understand yours?

If my heart burned with the flame of that love that devoured your heart, how contemptible earth would then seem to me, and how ardently I would long for heaven!

What is there for a heart overflowing with love of Jesus to desire in this life but the possession of Jesus?

If I were offered all of this world's goods so that I might be the happiest of men, I would say without ceasing: *"I desire to be freed from this life and to be with Christ, for that is the far better thing"* (Phil 1:23).

What do all the goods of this world amount to for the man who knows and loves Jesus?

Jesus is the supreme good, and contains in Himself everything else that is good.

What happiness to be with Jesus, this father who is so good, this friend so loving, this master so generous, this savior so lovable! To be with Jesus, to enjoy His presence, to love Him with my whole soul and for all eternity! Queen of heaven, can this earth and this world offer me anything to equal such happiness? Let my desire be fulfilled and the blessed place where He dwells open its arms to me! Jesus alone can make me fully happy!

But the longing to be united with Jesus by death finds me agitated by the fear my sins cause. Dear Mother, pray for me that I may hope in the infinite mercy of my redeemer.

Mary

Yes, my child, hope, and hope firmly. If Jesus is a judge to strike terror into us, He is also a Savior full of kindness.

Maintain always your fear of His judgment, but let hope and love overcome your fear.

Be afraid, but be even more loving. Be persuaded that you cannot better manifest your affection for Jesus than by greatly desiring to see Him soon in His glory and to leave behind this world where it is so easy to betray the fidelity you owe Him.

Trust in these sentiments and be sure, my child, that when death comes God will protect you against your enemies. At that moment I will ask Him to help you, for I always watch over my children, but especially at the hour of their death.

CHAPTER 19

LOVE OF GOD

The Believer

VIRGIN Mother, you died as a victim of Divine love. At the end, the love of God slew with a fiery dart the victim that had been prepared through so many centuries.

A soul so generous to God, so submissive to His will, so faithful and so holy, could not leave this body behind in any other way.

I am not surprised, then, to see you expire of love; I am surprised, rather, that love had not consumed you long before.

You came forth, pure and spotless, from the Creator's hand. Hardly had you come to know Him when you decided that love of Him would be your only aim. Your heart drew nourishment and life solely from the flame of love that pierced it through and through.

Throughout your life you had eyes only for that love. You referred everything to it: thoughts, sentiments, words, actions, fears, hopes, joys, and sorrows.

The more we know the infinite greatness and perfections of God, the more lovable we find Him and the more we love Him. But what creature ever knew Him better than you?

The hearts of the saints are full of such love, but the heart of Mary contained the very fullness of love itself. The Seraphim love greatly, but compared to the furnace of love in Mary's heart their love is but a spark.

Mother of pure love (Sir 24:24—Vulgate), I would have to love as you loved and still love, if I were to explain how greatly you loved.

You died of love, yet we do not live by love and we make no great effort to win at least the favor of dying of love!

Mary

My child, God made you to love Him. Can you be preoccupied with anything else?

How mournful those unhappy people should be who cannot love Him Who alone is their happiness in time and eternity!

Rouse yourself, my child, from the ill-fated spiritual sloth that has halted your progress on the paths of divine love. Do not stop now that I you have set out on the journey.

You fear sacrifices. But where there is no sacrifice there can be no love, and that love is suspect which comes to light only when there is nothing to suffer for the beloved.

Love ardently and courageously. Be ready to lose every possession except the grace of God. Be ready, too, to bear with every evil rather than commit the least sin.

When your will has yielded to the charm of love, nothing will seem impossible to you. *Love is as strong as death* (Song 8:6) and does not acknowledge difficulty.

You must correct your faults and master your passions. Love, therefore, and love will accomplish that task in a short time.

Love only what God loves. When you love any creature, love it as He wants you to love it. God alone can be loved without limitation.

True love requires perfect indifference toward all that is not God. It seeks Him alone and in all things.

My child, under the rule of such love you will be perfectly happy. The more you accept its commands, the more you will want them.

You will indeed have to suffer in its bonds, but you will find joy in the slavery love imposes.

Let love of God be your only treasure. Then even though you be poor in this world's goods, love will sustain you. When you come to die, you will be happy at having let love's inspirations be your guide.

For many, death is a moment of terror; for the Christian, who is filled with this love, it will be a time of consolation and sweetest peace.

Abandon yourself, therefore, to love of God. Trust in its guidance. Let it be your life, your all, and try to do everything out of love.

The Believer

As I listen to you, holy Virgin, I feel coming to life within me a great desire to let love of God be my guide.

My God, my heart wants You alone. If You do not find this heart completely unworthy of You, here it is. I give it to You and dedicate it entirely to You.

The desire I feel is the effect of the grace you have obtained for me, dear Mother, for without that grace and your help I could not love God.

Without the help of grace I could not love Him as I ought nor persevere in loving Him. Pray without ceasing that this love may be in me always!

But I am weak and I am aware of my inconstancy. But you, my Mother, also know it and have rightly reproached me for it. Protect me, and be my staff and support.

Away from me, mean and ephemeral things of this world! You are what causes my heart to die! I want to live forever. But, my God, does a life without Your love deserve the name of life?

Let this world complain that I have deserted it! It claims to be my servant, yet it has snatched true happiness from me. I will continue to despise it until it stops being the enemy of my love.

Virgin, perfect model of love, shall my heart forget to strive for that paradisal state in which, imitating your life on earth and in heaven, I shall love only my God and be confident of dying in His love and continuing to love Him throughout eternity?

CHAPTER 20

HEAVENLY GLORY AS OUR REWARD

The Believer

HOLY Virgin, you now possess the glory God, Who rewards in supreme fashion, prepared for you because of your virtues and merits. When shall I witness your glory? When shall I contemplate it and marvel at it along with the angels and saints? When shall I join

their great concert and sing the praises you
have deserved?

The high glory reserved for you in heaven
was not simply a favor Jesus wanted for His
mother but was your due because you corresponded to the graces and intentions of God.

If you had not cooperated effectively and
courageously with the graces your Divine Son
gave you, you would not have such a high
place in paradise.

Your holy life was your chief merit in the
eyes of God Who is the God of all holiness.

Mary

My child, no one enters heaven unless he
has first become holy on earth.

It is not to position, wealth, or talent that
God looks when He allows a man to enter the
dwelling of the blessed, but to the holy use a
man has made of these things and the merits
he has won during his life.

God *shows no favoritism* (Eph 6:9), but *will
repay everyone in accord with what his deeds
deserve* (Rom 2:6).

Those who are highest in God's kingdom
are those who were most virtuous and perfect
on earth.

God's judgments are unlike those of men.
Men usually judge by externals and appear-

ances; God alone passes true judgment on merit and virtue.

He has great rewards stored up for you, but He wants you to merit them. To this end He gives His helps and graces. If you use them well, He will keep His promises.

He will indeed be crowning the very gifts He has given you, but at the same time He will be rewarding you for your virtues and good actions.

He keeps an exact account of what is done for Him. Even if you give but a cup of water in His name, that cup of water will be rewarded.

How consoling it is, my child, to toil for a master who is so great, good, and generous!

The world rewards its servants poorly, but you can say: *I know the One in Whom I have placed my trust, and I am confident that He is able to guard until that Day what He has laid up for me* (2 Tim 1:12) in the hands of the master I serve. I look to His mercy for an eternal crown that will be the more splendid as my fidelity in serving Him on earth has been more careful and persevering.

Examine yourself now and make note of what you are doing to merit and obtain the prize set before you.

Where are your victories? What good works have you done? What virtues have you practiced? What merits can you present to God?

The Believer

I am shamed when I think that up to now I have done so little to merit heavenly rewards.

Mary

Do not be downcast, my child, for you can still win those rewards. Grace is summoning you; be faithful to its voice.

Pray, lament for your sins, work, suffer, sacrifice, walk the ways of the saints: then, like the saints, you will reach the goal of happiness.

The Believer

With your help and protection, I shall at last shake off the sloth I have lived in till now. With your help I shall try to make up by fervor for the barren years I must bemoan.

Watchfulness, tears, humility, self-denial, patience in trials—how magnificently all that would be rewarded by even a few moments of the bliss the saints enjoy forever with God!

But the Lord Whom I serve is worthy for His own sake of my making every effort to please Him.

I want to serve Him and try to please Him for His own sake more than for the infinite blessings He has in store as the reward of fidelity.

JESUS APPEARS TO MARY

At dawn on Easter Sunday Jesus rose from the dead and tradition tells us He appeared first to His Mother. She thus shared in the joy and glory of His triumph.

266

BOOK 4

*Our Sentiments toward the
Blessed Virgin*

CHAPTER 1

GREATNESS OF THE
MOTHER OF GOD

The Believer

WHATEVER our sentiments toward you, holy Virgin, they will never be what your greatness deserves. For that greatness will always exceed all the ideas we may form of it.

To speak worthily of you, we would have to have a grasp of all that is most admirable in grace, perfection, power, and glory.

It was Mary who gave birth to Jesus Who is called the Messiah (Mt 1:16). The Gospel which tells us of this fact does not spend time in singing your praises. For these few words are of themselves enough of a basis for any praise that could possibly be given you.

Your dignity as Mother of God means nothing less than a kind of affinity with the supreme Being Himself, and the result of the Divine Maternity is that you were brought into the greatest possible proximity to the godhead.

That dignity created a special covenant between you and God, and in that covenant you became Daughter of the Father, Mother of the Son, and Spouse of the Holy Spirit in an extraordinary way proper to you alone. In virtue of that covenant you are truly Queen of the world and of heaven.

To say that Jesus was born of Mary is to say that there is no one superior to Mary but God Himself.

Holy Virgin, the most splendid of the angels, in all his perfection, is only a servant in comparison with you. So great is the distance between him and you.

I judge your greatness by that of your Son, for His greatness is necessarily reflected in you. From the Son's excellence the Mother may be known.

I understand that the high privilege of being Mother of Jesus is the basis for all the graces it pleased God to heap upon you, and of all the privileges and prerogatives with which He loved to favor you. I understand that, being Mother of Jesus, you had a kind of right to all the treasures of grace to which Jesus holds the key, and an unconditioned power of intercession with Him. I understand, too, that certain general laws which are the punishment for original sin could not apply to the Mother of my God, a Mother so lovable and loved, a mother destined to be such by eternal decree, a Mother who gave God the life in which He redeemed us and who earned the title of Mediatrix of our salvation.

But how can I possibly grasp the greatness of your dignity, Mother of God?

Every aspect of the Mother of a God is so extraordinary that even the Seraphim must be satisfied simply to admire it. You yourself, in the presence of your cousin Elizabeth, summed up in a few words all that God had done for you: *God Who is mighty has done great things for me* (Lk 1:49). The Church herself for all the love she has for you and all her zeal for your glory, when she reflects that you carried in your womb the One Whom the heavens cannot contain, is forced to confess that she does not know what words to use in her attempt to express your praises.

Admirable Mother of my God, in your presence I am moved, in the very depths of my being, to intense and loving wonder.

When I consider your greatness and dignity I am seized by a holy fear and by a respect that thrusts me down, like one reduced to nothingness, at your feet.

CHAPTER 2

LIKENESS OF MARY TO JESUS

The Believer

WHEN I think, holy Virgin, of your birth, life, death, and heavenly glory, I find a likeness between you and Jesus that transports me with wonder.

You were united to your Son by the eternal decrees of providence. *"The Lord possessed me in the beginning of His ways,"* eternal Wisdom says of herself in the Scriptures; *"from eternity I was brought forth. When the Lord was laying the foundations of the world, I entered into His plans and intentions"* (Prov 8:22-23, 27-28).

These lines refer properly to Jesus, but the Church also applies them to you.

How many promises and prophecies, figures and symbols in the old law, point to you in pointing to Jesus!

Jesus was by His very nature sinless; by grace you were free of original sin and exempted from even the slightest actual sin.

The Word of God, when He was enclosed in your womb for nine months, was in a sense identical with you.

During His infancy you fed Him with your very substance, and it became His own.

During His hidden life He lived with you for thirty years: the same home, the same conditions of life, the same preoccupations, the same thoughts and feelings. During His years of preaching He shared with you as far as possible His labors and sufferings, and the insults and shame that were His lot.

Jesus was the humblest, the mildest, the most loving and patient of men. You were the humblest, the mildest, the most loving and patient of women.

In Jesus all the Divine uncreated perfections were united. You were the apex of all created perfections; so perfect were you that all the Angels and Saints vanish away in comparison with you.

Jesus made you so like Himself that you were a living image of Him.

Like Jesus, your body did not corrupt in the grave. He rose from the dead by His own power; you were raised up because of a special privilege He gave you.

Like Him, you went body and soul to heaven. There He is seated at the Father's right hand, and you sit beside Jesus.

Jesus is all-powerful because of what He Himself is. You are all-powerful because of the Son Who has made you the dispenser of His treasures. He is sovereign Lord of heaven and earth. You are the Queen of angels and men.

Wherever Jesus is adored, you too are honored.

There is no heart dedicated to His love that is not also entirely dedicated to you. There is no church built to His glory that does not contain an altar built in your honor.

The sweet name of Mary is on the lips and in the hearts of true believers, for it is inseparable from the name of Jesus.

In its sacred functions the Church frequently unites praise of you to the praise it offers Jesus. It celebrates the mysteries of your life as it celebrates those of the life of Jesus.

Jesus is king of the ages, author of grace, our advocate with the Father, God of mercy, God of all consolation, and Light of the world.

Together with the Church we acclaim you as Queen of the world, Queen of heaven, our advocate, mother of grace, mother of mercy, consoler of the afflicted, star that guides us through storms to the harbor of salvation.

We offer eternal thanks to Jesus for having granted you all the favors and privileges which such a Son could not but give to such a Mother.

Holy Virgin, my words here in your presence reflect the great glory that is yours, but they are also a delight to my heart and to the hearts of all who love you.

CHAPTER 3

MARY'S GLORY IN HEAVEN

The Believer

HOLY Virgin and Queen, you reign in heaven over the Patriarchs whose fidelity you surpassed, over the Prophets and Apostles whose constancy you left far behind you, over the Virgins whose purity cannot be compared with yours, over all the Saints whom you outdid in humility, over all the Angels whose obedience was less than yours, and over all the Seraphim than whom you were far greater in love.

I venerate and admire you as you sit upon your throne of light, where you are the refuge of sinners because your power with God is so great. You are the support of the just, the hope of the afflicted, the comfort of nations.

I bless the Lord for having exalted you to such glory and having decreed that even your body should share in it before the day of the general resurrection.

It was only right that a body so pure that God could deign to become a man in it should not be touched by the corruption of the grave.

But who can rightly conceive of this glory? If *eye has not seen, ear has not heard, nor has the human heart imagined what God has prepared for those who love Him* (1 Cor 2:9), how can we understand what He prepared for you who have loved Him more than all the Saints together?

The glory you now enjoy is proportioned not only to your high dignity but to your great merits as well.

To judge how great your glory should be we need only consider who this mother of God is.

But if the glory of the Saints is measured by their merits and your sublime dignity in heaven by your great virtues, we must say that in heaven you are by yourself an order apart, always infinitely less than God but always immensely above all that is not God.

It was fitting that she to whom Jesus had given authority even over Himself should have the right to command the Angels and Saints. How eagerly they vie in giving you the obedience and honor that is your due!

Enraptured by the queenly rule you exercise over them, they serve you with sentiments that could please even God Himself.

Ceaselessly they bless the Lord for the special privileges of grace He granted you; ceaselessly they bless Him for the sublime prerogatives of glory with which He honors you.

What acclamations of joy and exultation accompany the blessings they bestow upon you yourself! How tender their veneration for you!

How they long to see you loved and honored by all hearts on earth as in heaven!

Lovable Queen of the heavenly city, shall it be my good fortune to sing with the angels and saints your praises and those of your Son Jesus? Shall I sing the indescribable delights that are your inheritance?

Mary

My child, to urge yourself on to the battles you must fight in overcoming all the obstacles to your happiness, think of the eternal blessings God has prepared for you if you are courageous and persevering. Think often that the glory He bestows is an infinite recompense for all you must endure, a treasure worth infinitely more than your afflictions, a rest that makes up for all weariness, a consolation that infinitely outweighs all suffering.

God alone is great, and only He can bestow truly great recompenses. In hell there is divine punishment, in heaven Divine reward.

If you have the good fortune, my child, to save your soul, you will see the Lord. You will possess and love Him, and never grow weary of seeing, possessing, and loving Him, for though He is ever the same in Himself He is always new to the blessed.

In the delightful abodes of heaven there is pleasure without pain, joy without anxiety, rest without disquiet, peace without fear, enjoyment without boredom. There is no other will there, no other affections, but the will and affections of God. He is all in each. Each one exists in Him, each one becomes rich, powerful, and happy with Him and like Him.

My child, if you wish to attain this happiness, toil without wearying. Do not say: I have labored this much; I have won these victories; have I not done enough? *Whoever stands firm to the end will be saved* (Mt 10:22).

The Believer

Mary, after Jesus you are my hope and my life. Obtain for me constancy in God's service, and after this exile let me see your Son Jesus. If the grace of Jesus is a foretaste of heaven and lets the soul sense how lovable He is, what must be the joy of seeing and possessing Him as He is?

HAPPINESS OF ST. JOHN TO WHOM JESUS GAVE MARY AS A MOTHER. ALL CHRISTIANS SHARE THAT HAPPINESS

The Believer

MOTHER of my Savior, what must have been the happiness of St. John when the dying Jesus chose him to take His place! He became your son; you became his mother. Rightly indeed did the Gospel call him *the disciple whom Jesus loved* (Jn 19:26); his attachment to Jesus and his perseverance in following Jesus, together with you, until the end won him this extraordinary favor.

Could even this Divine Master have given him a more precious inheritance? How gratefully John must have received it!

He always had a profound respect for you and was fully submissive to you. He sought always to act in a way worthy of the favor Jesus had shown him.

And what signs of kind regard, what tokens of tender love you gave him! At every moment he felt how sweet it was to have you near.

Happy disciple of Jesus! Happy son of the most lovable and holy of mothers! I would buy your happiness with all the calamities earth can inflict, your glory with all its humiliations, your treasure with all its crowns.

Mary

When Jesus died, it was not only John who became my son. When Jesus said to him: *"Behold your mother,"* and to me: *"Behold your son"* (Jn 19:26), John represented you and all Christians.

Toward you, my child, I feel all the love a true and tender mother could have for a beloved child.

Try, then, to be, like John, a true child in your affection for me. Above all, try to deserve all your mother's tender love by living a sinless, holy life that will honor her.

The Believer

My mother, *if I forget you, may my right hand fail me. May my tongue stick to the roof of my mouth if I do not remember you* (Ps 137:5-6).

What a happiness for me that the very Mother of Jesus Himself should deign to be my mother as well and account me as one of her servants! Since in your great goodness you have agreed to be my mother, it is with great satisfaction of soul and immense gratitude that I will forever be your loving son.

To be Mary's son! How far better such a glorious name is than all the titles of honor that men seek!

You are my mother! What priceless blessings such an adoption will bring me! To be your son is to have hell itself fear me.

I have been so long ungrateful to my God that I deserve every punishment, and I admit that I have earned neither pardon nor grace. Yet, now that I am your son, I hope for everything from God's mercy.

You have shown yourself my mother by obtaining for me the grace of conversion to God's service. Obtain for me now the grace of perseverance as well. Show me the kindness of a mother who loves her son tenderly even when he is unworthy of that love.

My mother, grant yourself the consolation of seeing henceforth in me a child who, because he loves you and Jesus, is not unworthy of your love for him.

Chapter 5

LOVE FOR MARY MOST HOLY

THE esteem God has for any being is the only criterion we have for properly evaluating it. What He loves, we too must love.

To understand what we should think of Mary and how much we should love her, consider God's esteem of her and the proofs of His love that He gave her.

"Countless in number are My spouses," says the Holy Spirit, *"but only one have I adorned with all perfections"* (Song 6:7-8). The spouse who is loved in this extraordinary way by God must, after Him, have complete rule of our hearts and sentiments.

God's love for her led Him to grant her every privilege that would set her apart. So our love for Mary ought to set her apart from all else that we love after God.

God so loved her that He gave her the first place, after Himself, in heaven and on earth. Thus in heaven and on earth there is, after God, no being more worthy of our veneration and love. That is why all holy men have given her first place in their hearts, after Jesus.

The holy Fathers tell us that we but pretend to love the Son if we do not love the Mother too, for the two loves are inseparable.

The Fathers make love of Mary one of the surest signs of predestination and one of the most precious gifts of grace.

The love Mary herself has for us tells us what our love for her ought to be in return.

She observes our needs, suffers our afflictions, forestalls our desires, puts up with our faults, and forgets our ingratitude. How eager, then, we should be in showing a return of love!

Let us be careful to profit by the opportunities we have of pleasing her. Nothing seems too humble when her service is at stake, for indeed nothing is unimportant when it comes to serving the Mother of God, the Queen of the world.

Let us be prompt to do anything that pertains to her cult, anything that can contribute to making her loved and honored.

Let us carefully offer her each day the tribute of our praise and the homage of our hearts, and find our glory in being one of her professed servants.

We should frequently raise our minds and hearts, and find our glory in being one of her professed servants.

We should frequently raise our minds and hearts to her throne, that we may admire her greatness and perfections and ask her protection. In order to honor and imitate her virtues, let us give alms and do the other works of love, let us fast and practice other forms of self-denial.

We should receive the sacraments on her feastdays so as to celebrate them in a holier way, and, if we can, offer Mass at times in gratitude for the blessings with which God has enriched her.

Let us often visit shrines set up in her honor, and venerate her images and such persons and places as are specially dedicated to her.

We should eagerly assist, as far as we can, at public manifestations of devotion to her and at sermons dealing with her virtues, her prerogatives, and the devotion Christian hearts should have toward her.

These are the ways in which a child of Mary tries to give witness to his own love for her and to win her love ever more fully in return.

Mary, powerful protector and loving mother of men, you see in my heart a sincere determination to be faithful to these holy practices.

I thank the Lord for the sentiments of love for you that He inspires in me. That He gives them to me is a sure proof of His love for me.

I shall vie in fidelity to you with all those servants and children of yours whom I see to be more fervent in such practices.

Would that I might rival the angels themselves! But such happiness is reserved to the Blessed in heaven.

CHAPTER 6

ZEAL OF A CHILD OF MARY FOR HIS MOTHER'S GLORY AND INTERESTS

Mary

MY CHILD, I am your mother, and I give you constant proofs of it by the blessings I bestow. You are my child; as such, you honor me, invoke my help in temptations and trials, and hope for my intercession with Jesus.

But among the possible ways of showing me your love, there is one that you greatly neglect.

The Believer

Loving mother, tell me what it is, and I will try to fulfill my whole duty to you.

Mary

You do not try enough to win honor and glory for me. It even seems at times that you are reluctant to defend me against those who insult me.

You should imitate my concern for you by your zeal in defending my interests and in seeing to it that your mother is glorified, honored, and loved.

It is not enough to give your heart to me, next to Jesus. You must also take the opportunities offered you to win the hearts of others to me.

My child, look at the efforts heresy has made and still makes daily to destroy or weaken the veneration given me. You should, as far as lies in your power, undo the effects of such outrages.

The Believer

Yes, hell has always unleashed its powers against you, holy Virgin, and it has always hated the name of Mary, the name that is so venerable and delightful to the faithful.

You are the woman of whom the Lord spoke when the world was first created: *I will establish hostility between you and the woman, between your line and her line. Her offspring will crush your head and you will bruise his heel*" (Gen 3:15). Because Satan wants to destroy all men, he would have none of them turn to you. He wants to root out the high esteem the Church has for you and for your influence with the sovereign Lord of the universe.

What a glorious thing for Mary that only heretics rise up against her and that her only enemies are the enemies of Jesus!

Tower of David, from which a thousand bucklers hang (Song 4:4), the weapons of your enemies will always be trophies for you.

God will always raise up zealous defenders of your glory. *The gates of hell will not prevail against you* (Mt 16:18).

How grateful I should be to God for having let me be born within the Church where I am blest in knowing and loving you!

But if I love you, dear mother, I must defend your interests and take every opportunity to win glory for you. Henceforth, then, I shall exert myself to increase, as far as I can, the ranks of your servants. When occasion offers, I shall suggest to my relatives, friends, and acquaintances practices of devotion in your honor, and I shall consider it a delight to speak to them of you.

If I cannot by words revive in lukewarm hearts the love they ought to have for you, I shall try to do it at least by my example.

Above all, I shall never allow you to be spoken of in a derogatory way in my presence. Anyone who does not honor you does not himself deserve to be honored, and I want no one for my friend who is not your friend as well.

I shall ask God to touch with His grace the hearts of all men so that they may learn to know and love Jesus and, at the same time, to know and love her who is mother of them all.

How will men be unable to love her who from all eternity has been the object of love and delight for God Himself?

CHAPTER 7

MARY'S POWER WITH GOD
ON BEHALF OF MEN

MARY is the Daughter eternally loved by the Father, the Mother of the Son, and the Spouse of the Holy Spirit. Understand the meaning of these words and you will have some idea of her power.

As the spotless Daughter of the heavenly Father she is more perfect than all other creatures taken together. Her power over the heart of her Divine Father is unlimited.

He gives her now in heaven power over all the graces with which He enriches our world.

As true Mother of the Son in His manhood, will He not hear her?

By her prayers she can do all that the Son Himself does; that is how the holy Fathers speak of her.

To doubt that she has enough power with God to obtain the graces we need is to doubt that the Son honors His Mother.

Solomon said to Bathsheba: *"Ask it, my mother, for I will not refuse you"* (1 Ki 2:20). When Mary prays for us, she receives the same answer, for she has a greater claim on it than Bathsheba had.

When we pray for something through the intercession of the Saints, their love for the Lord and our confidence in them persuade Him to be favorable to us. But when we pray through the intercession of Mary, it is her high position and her dignity as God's Mother that speak in our favor.

Recall that God Himself chose to be subject to her on earth. Will He have less regard for her now that she reigns with Him in heaven?

He has entrusted to her, as it were, the general disposition of all His blessings and it pleases Him to give us a share of them through her.

Finally, if a tenderly loved wife can obtain everything she wants from her husband, Mary, who is Spouse of the Holy Spirit, can petition her Divine Spouse on our behalf and obtain even the greatest graces.

God has appointed her queen of heaven and earth and has given her a power suitable to her rank.

Of what value would the title of queen be to her if she could not help those in need and make them happy?

When the Saints petition God, He sometimes answers them with the most striking miracles. Will He be more reluctant to answer the prayers of her who is Queen of the Saints?

MARY CROWNED QUEEN OF HEAVEN

Mary is Queen of heaven and earth. She shares in the glory of her Son just as she shared in His sufferings on earth through which He redeemed the world.

Virgin, whom Angels and Saints alike praise, I am persuaded of your power with God and I place myself entirely under your protection. It is a sure protection that will never fail me, an efficacious protection that will overcome every obstacle, a universal protection from which no one is excluded.

Since I am an unworthy child of my Father and do not deserve to have Him hear me, I have chosen you to intercede with Him for me.

Mother of my God, watch over my actions and direct my steps always and everywhere, for everywhere there are spiritual and temporal dangers.

Protect me especially on that fateful day after which there is no more time to look forward to, no graces to hope for, and in that fearful and decisive hour that will end my earthly course and begin my eternity.

My trust in your protection does not mean that I may laze along until that last hour in guilty inactivity. It is not thus that your servants think of your protection. Helped by the graces Jesus gives me, I shall make your concerns my own and work with you so that I may some day reach the place of eternal happiness to which you wish to bring all who serve you faithfully.

CHAPTER 8

MARY'S HEARTFELT KINDNESS TO US

The Believer

HOLY Virgin, mother of mercy, we need only tell you of our wretchedness and needs and you turn to Jesus in our behalf. Could you fail to be concerned for us when you reflect that in your womb Jesus took the same mortal nature that we have?

Mother of Jesus, you do not forget His brothers, His members, His fellow heirs.

Whatever be the sad circumstances in which we find ourselves, you cannot refuse us your help, for your kindness is unlimited.

The annals of the Church offer countless examples of your great power and your watchful understanding.

You are the City of God and all praise you for the blessings you win for us. *"Glorious things are said of you"* (Ps 87:3), the Scriptures tell us.

We often complain about the many evils we must suffer in this life, and we do not reflect that we would have many more to endure if your prayers did not hold back God's justice in our regard.

We often feel unhappy, and the reason is that we do not think of asking you to pray God for us.

We do not think of you, even though the Church has taught us from our childhood to address you as "Consoler of the afflicted, and Help of Christians."

That is indeed what you are. Can anyone claim to have invoked you and not been heard? He would be an ungrateful man indeed!

If your intercession does not always obtain for us from God all the graces we want, that is for reasons into which we should not inquire. But your intercession always wins for us at least the grace of patience, submission, and resignation to God's will.

In creating you, Mary, God intended you to be our advocate, our refuge, our consolation, our mother. Therefore He made you a woman of immense compassion and mercy.

Jesus could not have dwelt so long within you without making your heart be in every way like His.

You are the image of the Divine model of mildness and kindness Whom you had before your eyes for thirty years, and, like Him, you love to do good.

Seated on the glorious throne to which God raised you in heaven, you imitate the mercy of

God Himself. He is far more ready to bestow on men, even the most ungrateful, His graces rather than His punishments.

Holy Virgin, in order to see how kind your heart is, I need only look at myself and the great benefits I have received from you.

In the hearts of those who love you there are so many proofs of your goodness that no argument is needed.

CHAPTER 9

RECOURSE TO MARY

Mary

MY CHILD, in whatever difficult situation you find yourself, invoke my aid and I will intercede for you.

If there is anything you want that is not contrary to God's glory and your own salvation, ask me and I will always be ready to hear you.

Do not ask for anything unless you also want God's will to be done. Any prayer made to me in that spirit will never be fruitless.

Many Christians ask me to obtain what they know is contrary to God's will.

Can they deceive themselves into thinking their prayers will be answered?

Others think of fuming to me only when they want earthly goods, but they are completely indifferent when it comes to God's graces.

If I pray for such people, it is not in order to obtain the harmful thing they ask for, but to obtain for them that which would be advantageous to them and which they do not think of requesting.

I ask for them the afflictions that will detach them from this world and urge them to think of heaven.

What you ought to ask of me before all is graces of conversion and salvation, graces whereby you may grow in virtue and win merit for heaven.

I always listen favorably to such prayers.

I do not ask temporal favors for those who invoke me, unless these may bring them genuine profit.

The successful outcome of a lawsuit or an abundant harvest may be the worst thing in the world for the person who asks it, for people who are prosperous often fail to think of eternity.

Many sick people ask me for a cure, but I request of God only the graces they need in their illness.

I am not the kind of mother who is blinded by feeling and fails to look for the true happiness of her children. My tender love for you, my child, will never lead me astray.

I intercede for you with Jesus only to obtain for you what is most useful in this life and the next.

Believe this and confidently ask my protection. Ask it in all your trials, whatever their nature be.

Such trials are frequent. Let my name, therefore, after the name of Jesus, be ever on your lips and written indelibly on your heart.

The Believer

Holy and lovable name of Mary! Name that no one utters confidently without being the better for it!

Happy the man who often recalls it with love, utters it devoutly, venerates it from the heart, and calls upon it often.

After the name of Jesus, that name that is *above all other names* (Phil 2:9), there is no other more worthy of respect, no other that is sweeter and dearer to the faithful than the name of Mary.

When the sinner invokes it, he feels a surge of hope in the Lord's mercy; the just man conceives a more ardent love; he who is tempted overcomes his own passions; he who is in tribulation feels consoled and inclined to be long-suffering.

After the name of Jesus, your name, Mary, will be my comfort in affliction, my counsel in doubt, my strength in the struggle, and my guide at every step I take.

CHAPTER 10

CONFIDENCE IN MARY

Mary

MY CHILD, you do not have perfect confidence in me. At times you are slow to call on me when you are in need, and at all times you seem unsure of my good will toward you.

I want you to have all the confidence in me that any son should have in his mother, knowing as he does her tender love and her goodness. Come to me always and everywhere, in all your spiritual and temporal needs, in difficulties of soul and body, in the difficulties of your relatives and friends.

Is it a sign of any great confidence in me if you turn to me only from time to time, on my feastdays, for example, as some Christians do?

You should imitate the Church which asks nothing of God without appealing to my intercession.

The Church has recourse to me as dispenser of the Lord's graces; let her conduct be the norm for yours, and, like her, have unfailing confidence in me, a confidence that is all-embracing, ardent, sweet, and affectionate.

Turn to God through Jesus, but turn to Jesus through His Mother. I am the surest way of reaching Jesus, of finding Him, and of receiving a warm welcome from Him.

The Believer

Queen of heaven, I acknowledge your power and goodness, but I fear that I am unworthy of you. Can a virgin so pure, so zealous for God's honor, and so perfect, turn to me in compassion?

Mary

My child, am I not the refuge of sinners? I intercede for all those who want to turn back to God's service and who call upon me with confidence.

Moved by my concern for their reconciliation, God has never said no to my prayer. For many sinners I am the only means left them and the only means God gives them of regaining His friendship. I have won pardon for sin, even enormous sins, for so many Christians. They asked my protection against God's justice, and I protected them until I won their reconciliation with their Judge.

Some sinners live stubbornly on in their sins while deluding themselves that I will win for them the grace of not dying in their sins.

That is presumptuous confidence and an insult to me. Others, however, groan beneath the weight of their sins and want to cast it off; they are aware of their weakness and put their trust and hope in me, praying that through my intercession I may win the grace of strength and forgiveness for them. Come! Draw near! I will not reject you but welcome you with love.

The Believer

Mother of my Lord, . . . the moment that the sound of your greeting reached my ears (Lk 1:43-44), all my disquiet vanished, and my confidence in you returned, stronger than ever.

To me you are like the dove that returned after the flood carrying an olive branch, the symbol of peace. Accept under your saving protection this sinner who is ashamed, deeply moved, and sorry for the sins of his lifetime, sins that he would like to expiate with his blood.

Obtain for me the grace to weep bitterly for the sins I have committed and to die rather than commit once again sins I so much detest. Through the holy Child of your womb, you won peace between God and men. Win peace for me as well, between me and my conscience, between me and my God.

Virgin, powerful and so full of kindness, how grateful I should be for all the blessings I receive from God through your intercession! Let all hearts be forever dedicated to you! Let all mouths voice the praises which heaven speaks to earth: "May Mary be loved and glorified!" and which earth echoes back to heaven: "May Mary be glorified and loved through all ages!"

CHAPTER 11

THE "HAIL MARY"

YOU recite this prayer daily when you address the Blessed Virgin. But do you take note of the glorious things it says of her and of the consolation and instruction it contains for you?

Before her altar you should sometimes make this prayer the subject of your meditation, for this will help you recite it with the respect and attention it calls for.

You greet Mary as "full of grace." Do you understand the greatness that is expressed in these few words? You say "The Lord is with you." God was indeed with Mary in a completely unique fashion in which no other being, not even the greatest saints, could share. In a quite special way He protected her and guided the powers of her soul in their exercise.

As you say these words, form in your heart a burning, sincere desire to share in the indescribable happiness of the Blessed Virgin.

What more can we desire, after all, than to have God with us? What more can we hope for? If we have God, what can sadden us?

Account yourself happy, along with Mary, because "blessed are you among women," that is, because she received many privileges which the Lord has given to no one else.

Tell her of the heartfelt joy that is yours because of the love God had for her and the praises heaped on her in heaven and on earth.

Then add, with St. Elizabeth: "Blessed is the fruit of your womb." Blessed indeed is the Son of Mary, and adored and glorified throughout the universe. Enjoy for a moment the pleasure such a thought brings to the soul that loves Jesus.

The Church next bids you ask the Blessed Virgin to pray for you who are a sinner. The Church would have you understand that because of your sins you do not deserve to be heard, whereas Mary will be heard if she prays for you. Yes, the Lord will hear her because she is His Mother. That is why the Church invokes her under that title which is so dear to her and so glorious in her eyes.

"Holy Mary, Mother of God." Your power with your Son is unlimited. Along with your goodness, that power is the basis of all my hope in you.

Finally, ask the Blessed Virgin to pray for you "now and at the hour of our death." Throughout life dangers to salvation are everywhere, and you need, therefore, a constant protection.

In the hour of your death your enemies will redouble their efforts to destroy you, and protection will be even more necessary than now.

The moment of death is a fearful one, but the servant of Mary can never die an outcast.

CHAPTER 12

SENTIMENTS OF CONFIDENCE IN MARY DURING LIFE

The Believer

HOLY Virgin, the enemies of my salvation surround me and try to snatch the grace and friendship of God from me. Protect me against their attacks and win victory for me!

Daughter of the God of armies, let a lightning-flash of your power strike among my enemies, and they will straightway flee from me.

Mother of the Lord of the winds and storms, say but a word in my behalf, and I shall be calm again.

Spouse of the Spirit of light and strength, obtain for me the grace of knowing and using the means that will successfully resist these terrible enemies!

In my confusion I throw myself into your arms as a frightened child throws himself into his mother's arms.

I am a great sinner, yet Jesus wants you to regard me as your child. This is the moment to let me see that you are truly a mother to me. I ask you to give me this favor, not out of love for me who am unworthy of your solicitude, but out of the love you have for your Son Jesus.

Even the rich of this world sometimes help the poor when they ask aid. Will you, who are Queen of heaven and earth, let go unheard the prayer of a needy man who anxiously calls upon your kindness?

As you pray for me lest I fall into the snares set by the enemies of my salvation, pray also, holy Virgin, that I may weep bitterly for my sins and win forgiveness for them.

Let my desire be fulfilled of serving no other master but Jesus. May I repent deeply of the sin I committed in serving the world which is His enemy.

Do not consider what I am of myself or what my sins have made me. Consider only what I am worth because of the blood that redeemed me. God wanted you to witness the death of Jesus on Calvary so that you might share His attitude to sinners and ask mercy for them.

It was when you shared the shame and pain of the crucified Jesus that He gave you to me as a mother, so that someday you might also have compassion on my wretchedness and need.

How many sinners who should have gone to hell are now enjoying heavenly happiness instead because you interceded for them! Obtain for me too the grace of repentance that you obtained for them.

It has never been known that you refused to listen to the prayer of a sinner who realized his sinfulness and turned to you in order to win forgiveness.

Mary, what a glorious thing it is for you that God should make somehow dependent on you the forgiveness of so many sinners! What I seek to win through your intercession will, if I obtain it, contribute still more to that glory.

Holy Virgin, make my cause your own so that I may persevere in fear and love of God. Win that grace for me. Not even by the greatest degree of virtue can I merit it; what then can I possibly hope for since I am nothing but weakness and inconstancy?

Your name, the sweet name of Mary, is the only thing that enables sinners to hope for the supreme evidences of friendship on God's part.

CHAPTER 13

SENTIMENTS OF CONFIDENCE IN MARY AT THE HOUR OF DEATH

The Believer

MOTHER of the Redeemer, it might well be that I am now at the end of my life, and therefore I ask even more insistently for your help. I see myself suspended as it were between heaven and hell. What will be my fate if you do not use your power with Jesus in my behalf?

In your hands He has placed the most precious graces for distribution to men. In your compassion, give them to me no less than to others.

At this hour I need them more than ever before.

Perhaps I am momentarily to appear before that judgment seat where I must give an account of my life. Speak for me before that moment comes! For the Mother of my Judge will surely obtain a favorable judgment for me.

Star of the sea, guide me through the storm that threatens to shipwreck me, and lead me safely to the harbor of salvation.

Heavenly light, break up the clouds which the spirit of darkness seeks to cast over my soul; calm the fear I feel when I think of the sins I have committed throughout life; obtain for me sincere repentance for my sins.

Model of every virtue, teach me vigorous faith, strong hope, and perfect love.

I thank you for all the goodness you have shown me throughout my life, even when I was most unworthy of it. Shall you refuse your protection now when my confidence in you is growing along with my growing need?

Loving Mother, most loving of all mothers, you will surely not abandon your dying child but help him to the last breath.

I am glad to die because it is Jesus' will that I should die. Despite my natural horror of death I die happy because I die under your protecting mantle.

Soon, I trust, I shall look directly upon my great, lovable, victorious, perfect Jesus; soon I shall marvel at you on your throne of light.

My death agony is approaching. Even if in that moment my lips can no longer ask for your help, my heart will still speak to you.

Over and over again I shall call with deep affection on the holy names of Jesus and Mary. My Jesus, accept all the sighs and movements of my heart during my agony, and all the other acts of love being offered to You and Your holy Mother.

Lord, have mercy, I dare not say "on Your servant," for, being such a great sinner, I do not know whether I shall be fortunate enough to please You at the judgment; but have mercy on me because I am *the child of your hand-maid* (Ps 116:16).

You have given me the grace of very great confidence in Mary throughout my life. I thank You because I feel my confidence redoubled in this hour that is so crucial for my salvation.

My God, God of mercy, I now ask You for a new favor: that I may be saved through the prayers of the Blessed Virgin, whom the Church bids us invoke at all times but especially at the hour of our death.

CHAPTER 14

DEVOTION TO ST. JOSEPH, HUSBAND OF THE BLESSED VIRGIN

TO CHOOSE St. Joseph as our special protector is to offer an especially valued proof of love to Mary most holy. We should have great esteem of this Saint, for God chose him to watch over the infancy of the Word made flesh and to be witness and protector of His Mother's virginity.

He kept guard over the true tabernacle of Israel; according to need, he transported the ark of the new covenant; he safeguarded the pledge of mankind's salvation and redemption.

What a glorious thing it was to have had authority during their earthly life over the Queen of heaven and earth and over the King of the ages Who alone is immortal and to Whom all glory is due!

In order to have an idea of his outstanding merit we need only consider that he was the husband of Mary. We can judge his virtues by hers, for God gave Mary a husband worthy of her.

Reflect also on the fact that the infant Jesus rested so often in Joseph's arms. What feelings this child who was God must be roused in his heart!

Joseph lived with Him Who is the source of all grace and with her who is as it were the channel of its distribution. What spiritual riches he must have received from them! All the virtues—patience, mildness, humility, love of neighbor and God—were his in the highest degree.

The Church has built churches to God in St. Joseph's honor. She has established feast-days for him and invites her children to use authorized practices of devotion to him and to consider him one of the most powerful protectors we have before God.

The name of Joseph is indeed invoked in a special way by the faithful since they often link it with the names of Jesus and Mary.

If we had wanted to obtain some special favor from Jesus and Mary while they were living at Nazareth, what more powerful mediator than Joseph could we have found? Do you think he has less power now?

Go to Joseph (Gen 41:55) and he will intercede for you. Whatever be the grace you ask, God will give it to you at his request.

Moreover, no matter what your state and condition are, these will provide you with reason for special confidence in Joseph.

The rich and those of high rank should realize, when they pray to him, that he was descended from the patriarchs and kings. The poor should recall that he does not scorn them for their obscure lives, since he himself lived in great need and toiled as a handworker all his life.

Virgins should remember that he preserved perfect virginity; married people, that he was head of the most venerable of all families; children, that he was guardian of Jesus and protected and guided Him in His childhood; priests, that he so often had the happiness of holding Jesus in his arms and that he offered the eternal Father the first blood shed by Jesus on the day of the circumcision; religious, that he sanctified the solitude of Nazareth by a complete rejection of the world and by giving himself wholly to Jesus and Mary.

Finally, let devout and fervent souls consider that, next to Mary, no heart ever loved Jesus with a more ardent and tender love than did the heart of Joseph.

Above all else, we should have recourse to Joseph when we wish to obtain the grace of a good death. The widespread view that Joseph himself died in the arms of Jesus and Mary has roused in the faithful a great confidence that through his intercession their own deaths may be as happy and consoling as his was. It is especially when they are dying that the faithful will gather the fruit of the devotion they had to this great Saint in their lifetime.

APPENDIX 1

Pope Paul VI

ON THE VALUE OF DEVOTION TO THE BLESSED VIRGIN

Christ is the only way to the Father,[1] and the ultimate example to Whom the disciple must conform his own conduct,[2] to the extent of sharing Christ's sentiments,[3] living His life and possessing His Spirit.[4] The Church has always taught this and nothing in pastoral activity should obscure this doctrine. But the Church, taught by the Holy Spirit and benefitting from centuries of experience, recognizes that devotion to the Blessed Virgin, subordinated to worship of the divine Savior and in connection with it, also has a great pastoral effectiveness and constitutes a force for renewing Christian living.

It is easy to see the reason for this effectiveness. Mary's many-sided mission to the People of God is a supernatural reality which operates and bears fruit within the body of the Church. One finds cause for joy in considering the different aspects of this mission, and seeing how each of these aspects with its individual effectiveness is directed toward the same end, namely, producing in the children the spiritual characteristics of the Firstborn Son. The Virgin's maternal intercession, her exemplary holiness and the divine grace which is in her become for the human race a reason for divine hope.

The Blessed Virgin's role as Mother leads the People of God to turn with filial confidence to her who is ever ready to listen with a mother's affection and efficacious assistance. Thus the People of God have learned to call on her as the Consoler of the Afflicted, the Health of the Sick, the Refuge of Sinners, that they may find comfort in tribulation, relief in sickness and liberating strength in guilt. For she, who is free from sin, leads her children to combat sin with energy and resoluteness. This liberation from sin and evil[5]—it must be repeated — is the necessary premise for any renewal of Christian living.

The Blessed Virgin's exemplary holiness encourages the faithful to "raise their eyes to Mary who shines forth before the whole community of the elect as a model of the virtues." It is a question of solid, evangelical virtues: faith and the docile acceptance of the Word of God;[6] generous obedience;[7] genuine humility;[8] solicitous charity;[9] profound wisdom;[10] worship of God manifested in alacrity in the fulfillment of religious duties,[11] in gratitude for gifts received,[12] in her offering in the Temple[13] and in her prayer in the midst of the apostolic community;[14] her fortitude in exile[15] and in suffering;[16] her poverty reflecting dignity and trust in God;[17] her attentive care for her Son, from His humble birth to the ignominy of the Cross;[18] her delicate forethought;[19] her virginal purity;[20] her strong and chaste married love.

These virtues of the Mother will also adorn her children who steadfastly study her example in order to reflect it in their own lives. And this progress in virtue will appear as the consequence and the already mature fruit of that pastoral zeal which springs from devotion to the Blessed Virgin.

Devotion to the Mother of the Lord becomes for the faithful an opportunity for growing in divine grace, and this is the ultimate aim of all pastoral activity. For it is impossible to honor her who is "full of grace"[21] without thereby honoring in oneself the state of grace, which is friendship with God, communion with Him and the indwelling of the Holy Spirit. It is this divine grace which takes possession of the whole man and conforms him to the image of the Son of God.[22]

The Catholic Church, endowed with centuries of experience, recognizes in devotion to the Blessed Virgin a powerful aid for man as he strives for fulfillment. Mary, the New Woman, stands at the side of Christ, the New Man, within whose mystery the mystery of man alone finds true light; she is given to us as a pledge and guarantee that God's Plan in Christ for the salvation of the whole man has already been realized in a creature: in her.

Contemplated in the episodes of the Gospels and in the reality which she already possesses in the City of God, the Blessed Virgin offers a calm vision and a reassuring word to modern man, torn as he often is between anguish and hope, defeated by the sense of his own limitations and assailed by limitless aspirations, troubled in his mind and divided in his heart, uncertain before the riddle of death, oppressed by loneliness while yearning for fellowship, a prey to boredom and disgust. She shows forth the victory of hope over anguish, of fellowship over solitude, of peace over anxiety, of joy and beauty over boredom and disgust, of eternal vision over earthly ones, of life over death.

Let the very words that she spoke to the servants at the marriage feast of Cana, "Do whatever He tells you,"[23] be a seal on our Exhortation and a further reason in favor of the pastoral value of devotion to the Blessed Virgin as a means of leading men to Christ. Those words, which at first sight were limited to the desire to remedy an embarrassment at the feast, are seen in the context of Saint John's Gospel to re-echo the words used by the people of Israel to give approval to the Covenant at Sinai,[24] and to renew their commitments.[25] And they are words which harmonize wonderfully with those spoken by the Father at the theophany on Mt. Tabor: "Listen to Him."[26]

(Devotion to the Blessed Virgin Mary, no. 57)

1 Cf. Jn 14:4-11
2 Cf. Jn 13:15
3 Cf. Phil 2:5
4 Cf. Gal 2:20; Rom 8:10-11
5 Cf. Mt 6:13
6 Cf. Lk 1:26-38; 1:45, 11:27-28, Jn 2:5
7 Cf. Lk 1:38
8 Cf. Lk 1:48
9 Cf. Lk 1:39-56
10 Cf. Lk 1:29,34; 2:19,33, 51
11 Cf. Lk 2:21-41
12 Cf. Lk 1:46-49
13 Cf. Lk 2:22-24
14 Cf. Acts 1:12-14
15 Cf. Mt 2:13-23

16 Cf. Lk 2:34-35, 2:49; Jn 19:25
17 Cf. Lk 1:48; 2:24
18 Cf. Lk 2:1-7 Jn 19:25-27
19 Cf. Jn 2:1-11
20 Cf. Mt 1:18-25; Lk 1:26-38
21 Cf. Lk 1:28
22 Cf. Rom 9:29, Col 1:18
23 Cf. Jn 2:5
24 Cf. Ex 19:8; 24:3, 7; Deut 5:27
25 Cf. Jos 24:24; Ezr 10:12; Neh 5:12
20 Cf. Mt 17:15

APPENDIX 2:

PRAYERS TO MARY

HAIL Mary,
full of grace,
the Lord is with you.
Blessed are you among women
and blessed is the fruit of your womb,
Jesus.
Holy Mary,
Mother of God,
pray for us sinners,
now and at the hour of our death.

We Fly to Your Patronage

WE fly to your Patronage,
O holy Mother of God;
despise not our petitions in our necessities,
but deliver us always from all dangers,
O glorious and blessed Virgin.

Partial indulgence.

Remember, O Most Gracious
Virgin Mary

REMEMBER, O most gracious Virgin Mary,
that never was it known
that anyone who fled to your protection,
implored your help or sought your intercession,
was left unaided.
Inspired with this confidence,
I fly to you, O Virgin of virgins, my Mother;
to you do I come,
before you I stand, sinful and sorrowful.
O Mother of the Word Incarnate,
despise not my petitions,
but in your mercy hear and answer me.

Partial indulgence.

Hail, Holy Queen

HAIL, holy Queen, Mother of mercy;
hail, our life, our sweetness and our hope.
To you do we cry,
poor banished children of Eve.
To you do we send up our sighs,
mourning and weeping in this valley of tears.
Turn then, most gracious Advocate,
your eyes of mercy toward us.
And after this our exile
show unto us the blessed fruit of your womb,
  Jesus.
O clement, O loving, O sweet Virgin Mary.

Partial indulgence.

Holy Mary, Help the Helpless

HOLY Mary,
help the helpless,
strengthen the fearful,
comfort the sorrowful,
pray for the people,
plead for the clergy,
intercede for all women consecrated to God;
may all who keep your sacred commemoration
experience the might of your assistance.

Partial indulgence.

The Angel of the Lord

a) *During the year* (outside of Paschal Season)

℣. The Angel of the Lord declared unto Mary,
℟. And she conceived of the Holy Spirit.
Hail Mary.

℣. Behold the handmaid of the Lord,
℟. Be it done unto me according to your word.
Hail Mary.

℣. And the Word was made flesh,
℟. And dwelt among us.
Hail Mary.

℣. Pray for us, O holy Mother of God,
℟. That we may be made worthy of the promises of Christ.

Let us pray. Pour forth, we beg You, O Lord,
Your grace into our hearts:

that we, to whom the Incarnation of Christ
Your Son

was made known by the message of an Angel,
may by His Passion and Cross
be brought to the glory of His Resurrection.
Through the same Christ our Lord.

Queen of Heaven

b) *During Paschal Season*

QUEEN of Heaven, rejoice, alleluia:
For He Whom you merited to bear, al-
leluia,
Has risen, as He said, alleluia.
Pray for us to God, alleluia.

℣. Rejoice and be glad, O Virgin Mary, alleluia.
℟. Because the Lord is truly risen, alleluia.

Let us pray. O God, Who by the Resurrection
of Your Son,
our Lord Jesus Christ,
granted joy to the whole world:
grant, we beg You,
that through the intercession of the Virgin
Mary, His Mother,
we may lay hold of the joys of eternal life.
Through the same Christ our Lord.

A partial indulgence *is granted to the faithful, who devoutly recite the above prayers according to the formula indi-
cated for the time of the year.*

It is a praiseworthy practice to recite these prayers in the
early morning, at noon, and in the evening.

Prayer to Mary, Queen of the Home

O BLESSED Virgin Mary,
  you are the Mother and Queen of every
  Christian family.
When you conceived and gave birth to Jesus,
human motherhood reached its greatest achieve-
    ment.
From the time of the Annunciation
you were the living chalice
of the Son of God made Man.
You are the Queen of the home.
As a woman of faith,
you inspire all mothers to transmit faith
to their children.

Watch over our families.
Let the children learn free and loving obedience
inspired by your obedience to God.
Let parents learn dedication and selflessness
based on your unselfish attitude.
Let all families honor you
and remain devoted to you
so that they may be held together
by your example and your intercession.

Our Lady of Fatima

O MOST holy Virgin Mary,
  Queen of the most holy Rosary,
you were pleased to appear to the children of
  Fatima and reveal a glorious message.

We implore you,
inspire in our hearts a fervent love
for the recitation of the Rosary.
By meditating on the mysteries of the redemp-
    tion
that are recalled therein
may we obtain the graces and virtues
that we ask,
through the merits of Jesus Christ,
our Lord and Redeemer.

Our Lady of Lourdes

O IMMACULATE Virgin Mary,
    you are the refuge of sinners,
the health of the sick,
and the comfort of the afflicted.
By your appearances at the Grotto of Lourdes
you made it a privileged sanctuary
where your favors are given to people
streaming to it from the whole world.
Over the years countless sufferers
have obtained the cure of their infirmities—
whether of soul, mind, or body.
Therefore I come with limitless confidence
to implore your motherly intercessions.
Loving Mother,
obtain the grant of my requests.
Let me strive to imitate your virtues on earth
so that I may one day share your glory in heaven.

Our Lady of Guadalupe

OUR Lady of Guadalupe,
mystical rose,
intercede for the Church,
protect the Holy Father,
help all who invoke you in their necessities.
Since you are the ever Virgin Mary
and Mother of the true God,
obtain for us from your most holy Son
the grace of a firm faith and a sure hope
amid the bitterness of life,
as well as an ardent love
and the precious gift of final perseverance.

Prayer of Dedication to Mary

VIRGIN full of goodness,
Mother of mercy,
I entrust to you my body and my soul,
my thoughts and my actions,
my life and my death.
O my Queen,
come to my aid
and deliver me from the snares of the devil.
Obtain for me the grace of loving
my Lord Jesus Christ, your Son,
with a true and perfect love,
and after Him, O Mary,
of loving you with all my heart
and above all things.

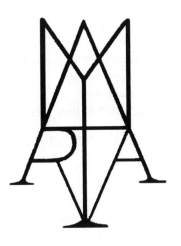

OTHER OUTSTANDING CATHOLIC BOOKS

HOLY BIBLE—St. Joseph Edition of the New American Bible. Large type with helpful Notes and Maps, Photographs, Family Record and Bible Dictionary **Ask for No. 611**

St. Joseph SUNDAY MISSAL—Complete Edition. All **3 cycles A, B, and C** with all Mass texts, illustrations, Prayers and Devotions. 1536 pages. **Ask for No. 820**

NEW TESTAMENT—St. Joseph Edition of the New American Bible Version. Large easy-to-read type, with helpful Notes and Maps. Photographs, and Study Guide. **Ask for No. 311**

Pocket Edition—legible type, illustrated. **Ask for No. 630**

Vest Pocket Edition—illustrated. **Ask for No. 650**

THE GLORIES OF MARY—By St. Alphonsus. Adapted and very readable modern version of a classic book about the Blessed Virgin. Large type, illustrated **Ask for No. 360**

DICTIONARY OF MARY—New and invaluable book that clearly sets forth the place of Mary in the Church and in the life of Catholics, her titles, authenticated apparitions, shrines, as well as Marian prayers and many other topics. **Ask for No. 367**

IMITATION OF CHRIST—By Thomas à Kempis. New edition. The one book that is second only to the Bible in popularity. Large type, illustrated. **Ask for No. 320**

FOLLOWING THE SAINTS—By Rev. W. van de Putte, C.S.Sp. Dialogues with more than 70 Saints plus inspirational prayers. Illustrated. 288 pages. **Ask for No. 336**

MARY DAY BY DAY—Minute meditations for every day of the year, including a Scripture passage; a quotation from the Saints; and a concluding prayer. **Ask for No. 180**

MINUTE MEDITATIONS FOR EACH DAY—By Rev. Bede Naegele, O.C.D. Short Scripture text, reflection, and prayer for each day. 365 illustrations in color. **Ask for No. 190**

EVERY DAY IS A GIFT—Introduction by Rev. F. Schroeder. Short daily meditations comprising a Scripture text, quotation from a Saint, and prayer. 365 illus. **Ask for No. 195**

WHEREVER CATHOLIC BOOKS ARE SOLD

ISBN 978-0-89942-330-2

90000

9 780899 423302